MOMENTS WITH

JESUS

FAMILY DEVOTIONAL

An Immersive Journey Through the Gospel of MARK

MOMENTS WITH

JESUS

FAMILY DEVOTIONAL

Eugene Luning

DESTINY IMAGE® PUBLISHERS, INC.
P.O. Box 310, Shippensburg, PA 17257-0310

"Publishing cutting-edge prophetic resources to supernaturally empower the body of Christ"

This book and all other Destiny Image and Destiny Image Fiction books are available at Christian bookstores and distributors worldwide.

For more information on foreign distributors, call 717-532-3040.

Reach us on the Internet: www.destinyimage.com.

ISBN 13 TP: 978-0-7684-7562-3

ISBN 13 eBook: 978-0-7684-7563-0

For Worldwide Distribution.

1 2 3 4 5 6 7 8 / 27 26 25 24 23

Contents

Introduction

Imagine an old man, walking across the one room of his little house—joints creaking and crackling as he walks—and then picture him pulling back the chair at his table, placing the other hand flat on the table's top, and gingerly letting himself down into the chair. In front of him is a piece of parchment, all he can presently afford, and he is preparing to write as much of a letter as he can fit on that one sheet, front and back.

But even before he begins, he is lost in a memory: a day from his youth. In it, he had just come in from fishing with his brother and his father; their two partners, also brothers, were beached down the way. With the sun coming over the hills, our young friend then walked north out of the harbor, just to stretch his legs and clear his mind. The morning was cool, but warming. A breath of a gust kept blowing up off the water.

As an old man, he can't remember how long he'd walked, but he would always remember what he saw when he returned...

His brother was leaning against their boat, looking out to sea. One of their partners was out in the deeps, accompanied by a Stranger whom they couldn't make out. And, strangely enough, the two of them looked to be preparing to cast out a net. In broad daylight. And nowhere near any of their usual spots.

Then down, down, down went the net and then, almost as suddenly as was humanly imaginable, the whole boat began listing to starboard, as if dragged down *by* that net. And now he saw his friend, his partner, turning to shout for their help, gesturing them to come as quickly as possible so that they wouldn't capsize.

And so out they went, our young friend and his brother, rowing with all their might, until they drew up, port to starboard, and began pulling on that net with all their strength. But even in the midst of these exertions, our friend couldn't help but glance at the face of the Stranger in the other boat. The Man was laughing, grinning from ear to ear at this absurd catch of fish.

And almost as if He'd felt the young man's eyes gazing upon Him, He suddenly looked right at him and their eyes locked. This was the moment when everything changed for our friend, John.

Now an old man, sitting at the writing table in the one room of his little house, he laughs aloud and begins to write his letter:

We are writing to you about something which has always existed yet which we ourselves actually saw and heard: something which we had an opportunity to observe closely and even to hold in our hands, and yet, as we know now, was something of the very Word of life himself! For it was life which appeared before us: we saw it, we are eye-witnesses of it, and are now writing to you about it. It was the very life of all ages, the life that has always existed with the Father, which actually became visible in person to us mortal men. We repeat, we really saw and heard what we are now writing to you about (1 John 1:1-3 PNT).

The purpose of this devotional is to awaken your family's hearts to encountering Jesus just like the apostle John—and Peter, Andrew, and James—once did. For Jesus, the One who "has always existed," *still* exists; He *still* desires to have a face-to-face, heart-to-heart relationship with *you*. He wants *you* to see and hear and "observe closely," "even to hold in [*your*] hands" the experience of knowing the Word of Life personally. He wants *you* and your family to feel like "eye-witnesses" of the Gospels—to know with confidence the "life that has always existed with the Father."

My friends, Life Himself wants to know you—and your family! He wants to draw your heart into the middle of the Gospel story!

As a follow-up to the *Moments with Jesus Encounter Bible*, I want to offer you something my own family has enjoyed at our own mealtimes. In short, simple segments from the Book of Mark (the earliest of the four Gospels), we like to read aloud a text each night and then quiz ourselves about the *Who-What-When-Where-Why-How* of what happened. Then, from there, we open our hearts about what we're noticing of Jesus in the passage: how He's revealing Himself, by His Spirit, to each of us personally. These conversations take only a few short minutes, and yet the day-by-day, mealtime-by-mealtime experience has been so enlivening for all of us.

I'd like to invite you on the same journey alongside Jesus!

As you'll see, I've already broken out the sections. First there is the scripture passage. Then the "Let's remember together what we read" section where I offer you a curated *Who-What-When-Where-Why-How* walk-through (including the answers!). Then, in the "Questions for us to ponder together," I offer one or two additional open-ended, "opening up our hearts" sort of questions for your family to linger with. My goal is that every reader, every family, will transit slowly through the Gospel of Mark, learning to listen, ponder, discuss—*and encounter Jesus!*

What do you say? Should we get started—*with Him?*

Eugene Luning
Colorado Springs, Colorado

Chapter 1

John the Baptist Prepares the Way

Mark 1:1-8

¹ *The beginning of the Good News of Jesus Christ, the Son of God.*

² *As it is written in the prophets,*

"Behold, I send my messenger before your face, who will prepare your way before you. ³ *the voice of one crying in the wilderness, 'Make ready the way of the Lord! Make his paths straight!'"*

⁴ *John came baptizing in the wilderness and preaching the baptism of repentance for forgiveness of sins.* ⁵ *All the country of Judea and all those of Jerusalem went out to him. They were baptized by him in the Jordan river, confessing their sins.* ⁶ *John was clothed with camel's hair and a leather belt around his waist. He ate locusts and wild honey.* ⁷ *He preached, saying, "After me comes he who is mightier than I, the thong of whose sandals I am not worthy to stoop down and loosen.* ⁸ *I baptized you in water, but he will baptize you in the Holy Spirit."*

Let's remember together what we read...

- Who is the "Good News" all about? *Jesus.*

- What were some of the things the Old Testament prophet said about John the Baptist? *He would come "before" Jesus. He would "prepare the way." He would* be a *"voice in the wilderness."* He would *"make ready the way of the Lord"* and *"make his paths straight."*

- What are the two things John the Baptist was up to, out there in the wilderness? *Baptizing and preaching repentance and forgiveness of sins.*

- Who went out to see what John was all about? *Practically everyone—folks from all over Judea and great crowds from Jerusalem.*

- What did they do before they were baptized? *Confessed their sins.*

- What was the name of the river where John did his baptizing? *The Jordan.*

- What was John the Baptist wearing? *Camel's hair and a leather belt.*

- What was he eating? *Locusts and wild honey.*

- What did John the Baptist say about Jesus? *That He was mightier than him; that he (John) didn't feel worthy of Him; that He would baptize people with the Holy Spirit.*

Questions for us to ponder together...

1. What is something that sticks out to you in this passage?

2. What will you remember?

Chapter 2

Jesus Is Baptized, Then Tempted

Mark 1:9-13

⁹ *In those days, Jesus came from Nazareth of Galilee, and was baptized by John in the Jordan.* ¹⁰ *Immediately coming up from the water, he saw the heavens parting and the Spirit descending on him like a dove.* ¹¹ *A voice came out of the sky, "You are my beloved Son, in whom I am well pleased."*

¹² *Immediately the Spirit drove him out into the wilderness.* ¹³ *He was there in the wilderness forty days, tempted by Satan. He was with the wild animals; and the angels were serving him.*

Let's remember together what we read...

- Where did Jesus come from? *Nazareth, a town in Galilee.*

- Where was He baptized by His older cousin, John the Baptist? *In the Jordan River.*

- What happened after Jesus was baptized? *The heavens opened up; the Holy Spirit came flying down, looking like a dove; a Voice spoke from the sky.*

- What did the Voice say? *"You are my beloved Son, in whom I am well pleased."*

- Then where did Jesus go? *Out into the wilderness.*

- Who sent Him out to the wilderness? *The Holy Spirit.*

- How long did He stay out there? *Forty days.*

- What was happening to Him while He was out there? *He was tempted by satan.*

- Who else was out there with Him? *Wild animals and angels, who served Him.*

Questions for us to ponder together...

1. Was there something that caught your attention about what we read?

2. Why?

Chapter 3

Jesus Begins His Ministry and Chooses His First Disciples

Mark 1:14-20

¹⁴ *Now after John was taken into custody, Jesus came into Galilee, preaching the Good News of God's Kingdom,* ¹⁵ *and saying, "The time is fulfilled, and God's Kingdom is at hand! Repent, and believe in the Good News."*

¹⁶ *Passing along by the sea of Galilee, he saw Simon and Andrew, the brother of Simon, casting a net into the sea, for they were fishermen.* ¹⁷ *Jesus said to them, "Come after me, and I will make you into fishers for men."*

¹⁸ *Immediately they left their nets, and followed him.*

¹⁹ *Going on a little further from there, he saw James the son of Zebedee, and John his brother, who were also in the boat mending the nets.* ²⁰ *Immediately he called them, and they left their father, Zebedee, in the boat with the hired servants, and went after him.*

Let's remember together what we read...

- What happened before Jesus left and went elsewhere? *John was arrested.*

- Where did Jesus go? *Into the Galilee region.*

- What did He do first? *Preached the Good News of the Kingdom of God.*

- What was His very first message? *"The time is fulfilled, and God's Kingdom is at hand! Repent, and believe in the Good News."*

- While He was walking along the seashore, who did Jesus see? *Simon and Andrew.*

- What were those two doing? *Casting out a fishing net.*

- What did Jesus say to them? *"Come after me, and I will make you into fishers for men."*

- And what did Simon and Andrew do? *Left everything and followed Jesus.*

- Then who did Jesus see? *James and John.*

- What were they doing? *Mending their fishing nets.*

- When Jesus called them, what did they do? *Left everything and followed Him.*

Questions for us to ponder together...

1. What was your favorite thing about what we just read?

2. How do you imagine what happened in your own mind?

Chapter 4

Jesus Casts Out a Demon in the Synagogue

Mark 1:21-28

²¹ *They went into Capernaum, and immediately on the Sabbath day he entered into the synagogue and taught.* ²² *They were astonished at his teaching, for he taught them as having authority, and not as the scribes.* ²³ *Immediately there was in their synagogue a man with an unclean spirit, and he cried out,* ²⁴ *saying, "Ha! What do we have to do with you, Jesus, you Nazarene? Have you come to destroy us? I know you who you are: the Holy One of God!"*

²⁵ *Jesus rebuked him, saying, "Be quiet, and come out of him!"*

²⁶ *The unclean spirit, convulsing him and crying with a loud voice, came out of him.* ²⁷ *They were all amazed, so that they questioned among themselves, saying, "What is this? A new teaching? For with authority he commands even the unclean spirits, and they obey him!"* ²⁸ *The report of him went out immediately everywhere into all the region of Galilee and its surrounding area.*

Let's remember together what we read...

- What town did Jesus and His friends go to? *Capernaum.*
- On the Sabbath day, where did they go? *Into the synagogue.*
- Did Jesus sit in the back row? *No.*
- In fact, what did Jesus immediately do? *Went up front and taught.*
- How did the people in the synagogue react to Jesus' teaching? *They were astonished at His authority, power.*
- Then what happened? *A man with an unclean spirit entered and started yelling at Jesus.*
- What were the things the demon-possessed man shouted at Jesus? *"What do we have to do with you? Have you come to destroy us? I know who you are: the Holy One of God."*
- What did Jesus say in return? *"Be quiet, and come out of him!"*
- What happened to the man? *He convulsed (shook violently), cried out, and the unclean spirit left him.*
- How did the people in the synagogue react to this freeing? *They were amazed.*
- What did they say to themselves? *"What is this? A new teaching? For with authority he commands even the unclean spirits, and they obey him!"*
- Did the people from the synagogue stay quiet about Jesus? *No! They talked about Him everywhere.*

Questions for us to ponder together...

1. If you'd been there that day, what would've been most memorable to you?
2. What would've stayed in your mind afterward?

Chapter 5

Jesus Heals a Woman and Her Whole Town

Mark 1:29-34

²⁹ *Immediately, when they had come out of the synagogue, they came into the house of Simon and Andrew, with James and John.* ³⁰ *Now Simon's wife's mother lay sick with a fever, and immediately they told him about her.* ³¹ *He came and took her by the hand and raised her up. The fever left her immediately, and she served them.*

³² *At evening, when the sun had set, they brought to him all who were sick and those who were possessed by demons.* ³³ *All the city was gathered together at the door.* ³⁴ *He healed many who were sick with various diseases and cast out many demons. He didn't allow the demons to speak, because they knew him.*

Let's remember together what we read...

- Where were Jesus and His friends leaving from, at the beginning? *The synagogue.*
- From last time, what had just happened in that place? *Jesus had been teaching, then a man came in with an unclean spirit, and Jesus set him free.*
- Where did Jesus go next? *To the house of Simon and Andrew.*
- Who was sick with a fever in that house? *Simon's wife's mother, i.e. Simon Peter's mother-in-law.*
- What did Jesus do? *Walked in, took her hand, and lifted her up. She was immediately healed by His touch.*
- What did she do after being healed? *Began serving Jesus and these houseguests.*
- That evening, what happened next? *The townspeople of Capernaum brought Jesus everyone who was sick and those possessed by demons.*
- Who did Jesus heal? *Everyone who came.*

Questions for us to ponder together...

1. What is one thing that you learned about Jesus— about His personality and power—from this passage?
2. What is He like, based on what we just read?

Chapter 6

Jesus, His Father, and His Purpose

Mark 1:35-39

[35] *Early in the morning, while it was still dark, he rose up and went out, and departed into a deserted place, and prayed there.* [36] *Simon and those who were with him searched for him.* [37] *They found him and told him, "Everyone is looking for you."*

[38] *He said to them, "Let's go elsewhere into the next towns, that I may preach there also, because I came out for this reason."* [39] *He went into their synagogues throughout all Galilee, preaching and casting out demons.*

Let's remember together what we read...

- What time of day did this section start with? *Early in the morning, while it was still dark.*

- What did Jesus do first? *Got up and went out alone, found a deserted place, and spent time talking to His heavenly Father.*

- Who came looking for Jesus? *Simon and the other disciples.*

- What did they say to Jesus when they found Him? *"Everyone is looking for you."*

- Somewhat surprisingly, what did Jesus say in response? *"Let's go elsewhere into the next towns"— meaning, away from the curious crowds—"that I may preach there also, because I came out for this reason."*

- Where did Jesus go? *All throughout the Galilee region.*

- In all the towns, where did He often go first? *Into their local synagogues.*

- What did He do while He traveled around? *Preached and cast out demons.*

Questions for us to ponder together...

1. What about Jesus are you more interested in after looking at these verses?

2. Did anything surprise you?

Chapter 7

Jesus and the Man with Leprosy

Mark 1:40-45

⁴⁰ *A leper came to him, begging him, kneeling down to him, and saying to him, "If you want to, you can make me clean."*

⁴¹ *Being moved with compassion, he stretched out his hand, and touched him, and said to him, "I want to. Be made clean."* ⁴² *When he had said this, immediately the leprosy departed from him and he was made clean.* ⁴³ *He strictly warned him and immediately sent him out,* ⁴⁴ *and said to him, "See that you say nothing to anybody, but go show yourself to the priest and offer for your cleansing the things which Moses commanded, for a testimony to them."*

⁴⁵ *But he went out, and began to proclaim it much, and to spread about the matter, so that Jesus could no more openly enter into a city, but was outside in desert places. People came to him from everywhere.*

Let's remember together what we read...

- Who, in this account, came right up to Jesus? *A man with leprosy.*

- What did the man with leprosy do when he saw Jesus? *Knelt before Him, begging for healing, and said, "If you want to, you can make me clean."*

- Did Jesus want to? *Yes!*

- How did Jesus feel toward the man? *Moved with compassion.*

- What did Jesus do? *Reached out His hand and touched his leprous skin.*

- What happened? *The man was immediately healed; he was made totally clean.*

- What did Jesus tell him to do? *To tell no one; to only show himself to the priest and make the offerings required by Moses in the Old Testament.*

- What did the healed man do instead? *Told absolutely everyone!*

- What did this mean for Jesus? *People became so curious that He had to be quiet when coming into cities, and He started spending more time in desert places.*

- Did more or less people now come to Him? *Far more.*

- Where did they come from? *From everywhere.*

Questions for us to ponder together...

1. How would you describe Jesus' heart for the people around Him?

2. Would He make a good friend?

Chapter 8

Jesus and the Paralyzed Man

Mark 2:1-12

² When he entered again into Capernaum after some days, it was heard that he was at home. ² Immediately many were gathered together, so that there was no more room, not even around the door; and he spoke the word to them. ³ Four people came, carrying a paralytic to him. ⁴ When they could not come near to him for the crowd, they removed the roof where he was. When they had broken it up, they let down the mat that the paralytic was lying on. ⁵ Jesus, seeing their faith, said to the paralytic, "Son, your sins are forgiven you."

⁶ But there were some of the scribes sitting there and reasoning in their hearts, ⁷ "Why does this man speak blasphemies like that? Who can forgive sins but God alone?"

⁸ Immediately Jesus, perceiving in his spirit that they so reasoned within themselves, said to them, "Why do you reason these things in your hearts? ⁹ Which is easier, to tell the paralytic, 'Your sins are forgiven;' or to say, 'Arise, and take up your bed, and walk?' ¹⁰ But that you may know that the Son of Man has authority on earth to forgive sins"—he said to the paralytic—¹¹ "I tell you, arise, take up your mat, and go to your house."

¹² He arose, and immediately took up the mat and went out in front of them all, so that they were all amazed and glorified God, saying, "We never saw anything like this!"

Let's remember together what we read...

- What town did Jesus come back to, at the beginning? *Capernaum.*

- Where did Jesus go there? *Into someone's house in the village.*

- What did He do? *Began speaking to them.*

- How many people were inside the house? *Lots—there was no room for anyone else.*

- Four people then came along, carrying who? *A friend who was paralyzed—who couldn't walk.*

- Were they able to get in the house through the door? *No!*

- So what did they do? *Took their paralyzed friend up on the top of the house, tore open the roof, and let down his mat right in front of Jesus.*

- What did Jesus say to the paralyzed man first? *"Son, your sins are forgiven you."*

- Did the religious leaders in the room like that? *No. They thought he was speaking "blasphemy," meaning they thought He was pretending to be God.*

- Did Jesus hear the religious leaders say this? *No. He actually **read their minds** from across the room!*

- And what did Jesus say to the religious leaders? *"Why are you thinking that? Which is easier. To say, 'Your sins are forgiven' or to heal this man's paralyzed body?"*

- And then what did Jesus do? *Healed the man.*

- What did the healed man do? *He just walked right out!*

- How did everyone react to the healing? *They were amazed and glorified God.*

Questions for us to ponder together...

1. What is your favorite thing about what we just read?

2. How do you imagine what happened in your own mind?

Chapter 9

Jesus, the Crowds, Levi, and Levi's Friends

Mark 2:13-17

[13] *He went out again by the seaside. All the multitude came to him, and he taught them.* [14] *As he passed by, he saw Levi the son of Alphaeus sitting at the tax office. He said to him, "Follow me." And he arose and followed him.*

[15] *He was reclining at the table in his house, and many tax collectors and sinners sat down with Jesus and his disciples, for there were many, and they followed him.* [16] *The scribes and the Pharisees, when they saw that he was eating with the sinners and tax collectors, said to his disciples, "Why is it that he eats and drinks with tax collectors and sinners?"*

[17] *When Jesus heard it, he said to them, "Those who are healthy have no need for a physician, but those who are sick. I came not to call the righteous, but sinners to repentance."*

Let's remember together what we read...

- After leaving the house where the paralyzed man was healed, where did Jesus go next? *Out by the seashore of the Sea of Galilee.*

- Who came along with Him? *Huge crowds of people.*

- What did Jesus do for the crowds? *Taught them.*

- Later, while He was walking through the town, who did Jesus notice? *Levi, the tax collector.*

- What did Jesus say to him? *"Follow me."*

- What did Levi do? *Got up and followed Jesus.*

- Where did Jesus go next? *To Levi's house for a meal.*

- Who else was there? *More tax collectors and people others considered to be "sinners," as well as Jesus and His disciples, plus some of the religious leaders.*

- Seeing the kind of people around Jesus, what did the religious leaders say? *"Why is it that he eats and drinks with tax collectors and sinners?"*

- How did Jesus answer this? *By saying that these are the exact kind of people He came for; that He is interested not in the self-righteous, but in the sinners who are ready to repent.*

Questions for us to ponder together...

1. Who in this passage do you feel like is you: the curious crowds; Levi, the tax collector; Levi's friends; Jesus' disciples; the religious leaders?

2. Where do you picture yourself within these scenes?

Chapter 10

Jesus and the New Covenant

Mark 2:18-22

[18] *John's disciples and the Pharisees were fasting, and they came and asked him, "Why do John's disciples and the disciples of the Pharisees fast, but your disciples don't fast?"*

[19] *Jesus said to them, "Can the groomsmen fast while the bridegroom is with them? As long as they have the bridegroom with them, they can't fast.* [20] *But the days will come when the bridegroom will be taken away from them, and then they will fast in that day.* [21] *No one sews a piece of unshrunk cloth on an old garment, or else the patch shrinks and the new tears away from the old, and a worse hole is made.* [22] *No one puts new wine into old wineskins; or else the new wine will burst the skins, and the wine pours out, and the skins will be destroyed; but they put new wine into fresh wineskins."*

Let's remember together what we read...

- Who are we told are the ones who were fasting? *John the Baptist's disciples and the Pharisees.*

- What did they come to Jesus to ask? *"Why are we fasting—and your disciples don't?"*

- What kind of celebration does Jesus then talk about when answering? *A wedding.*

- And who is Jesus saying He Himself is? *The groom—the one getting married.*

- In His answer to them, when does Jesus say His disciples *will* fast? *After He is "taken away."*

- What are the two pictures Jesus uses to explain the arrival of the New Covenant? *The patches on the garment; the new wine and the wineskins.*

- What do you think Jesus means with these pictures? *That He has come to bring something totally new that requires our hearts to be made new too. That we cannot put the new thing into something that is unchanged and old.*

Questions for us to ponder together...

1. What do you like about the way that Jesus speaks?

2. What are you taking to heart from what He said in this passage?

Chapter 11

Jesus and the Sabbath: Part One

Mark 2:23-28

²³ *He was going on the Sabbath day through the grain fields; and his disciples began, as they went, to pluck the ears of grain.* ²⁴ *The Pharisees said to him, "Behold, why do they do that which is not lawful on the Sabbath day?"*

²⁵ *He said to them, "Did you never read what David did when he had need and was hungry—he, and those who were with him?* ²⁶ *How he entered into God's house at the time of Abiathar the high priest, and ate the show bread, which is not lawful to eat except for the priests, and gave also to those who were with him?"*

²⁷ *He said to them, "The Sabbath was made for man, not man for the Sabbath.* ²⁸ *Therefore the Son of Man is lord even of the Sabbath."*

Let's remember together what we read...

- What day of the week did this happen on? *The Sabbath (for Jewish people, this was Saturday).*

- Where were Jesus and His friends walking? *Through the grain fields.*

- What did Jesus' friends begin to do? *To pluck and to snack on some of the grain.*

- Who was *also* walking through those grainfields, perhaps spying on Jesus? *The Pharisees.*

- What did they say to Jesus? *"Why are your disciples breaking the Law?"*

- Who did Jesus remind them of from the Old Testament? *David.*

- And Jesus reminded them of David doing what? *Going into God's house and eating the holy bread, which was absolutely not allowed.*

- What is Jesus trying to teach the Pharisees—and His friends? *That the Sabbath was made for us, for rest, for worship; we were not made to fear or worship the Sabbath itself.*

- What is an interesting name Jesus uses to describe Himself? *The "Son of Man."*

Questions for us to ponder together...

1. If Jesus was with us in person this next Sunday, how might He like to spend the day with us?

2. What would He consider to be a perfect sort of Sabbath together?

Chapter 12

Jesus and the Sabbath: Part Two

Mark 3:1-6

³ *He entered again into the synagogue, and there was a man there who had his hand withered.* ² *They watched him, whether he would heal him on the Sabbath day, that they might accuse him.* ³ *He said to the man who had his hand withered, "Stand up."* ⁴ *He said to them, "Is it lawful on the Sabbath day to do good or to do harm? To save a life or to kill?" But they were silent.* ⁵ *When he had looked around at them with anger, being grieved at the hardening of their hearts, he said to the man, "Stretch out your hand." He stretched it out, and his hand was restored as healthy as the other.* ⁶ *The Pharisees went out, and immediately conspired with the Herodians against him, how they might destroy him.*

Let's remember together what we read...

- Where did Jesus enter in, yet again? *The synagogue.*

- Who, in particular, was in the synagogue that day? *A man with a withered hand.*

- Who was watching Jesus especially closely? *The Pharisees.*

- What were they themselves watching for? *To see if He'd heal on the Sabbath day.*

- What did Jesus say to the man with the withered hand? *"Stand up."*

- Then what did He say to the Pharisees? *In essence, "Is it good, on the Sabbath day, to do good or to do bad? To save a person or to harm a person?"*

- How did Jesus feel toward the religious leaders? *Angry, "grieved."*

- What did He next say to the man with the withered hand? *"Stretch out your hand."*

- And what happened? *He was healed instantly!*

- And what did the Pharisees do? *Went out and started plotting how to harm or even kill Jesus.*

Questions for us to ponder together...

1. What do we think life was like for "the man with the withered hand" before that day?

2. How would he have felt about Jesus and talked about Jesus *after* that day?

Chapter 13

Jesus, the Crowds, and the Power of the Kingdom

Mark 3:7-12

7 Jesus withdrew to the sea with his disciples; and a great multitude followed him from Galilee, from Judea, 8 from Jerusalem, from Idumaea, beyond the Jordan, and those from around Tyre and Sidon. A great multitude, hearing what great things he did, came to him. 9 He spoke to his disciples that a little boat should stay near him because of the crowd, so that they wouldn't press on him. 10 For he had healed many, so that as many as had diseases pressed on him that they might touch him. 11 The unclean spirits, whenever they saw him, fell down before him and cried, "You are the Son of God!" 12 He sternly warned them that they should not make him known.

Let's remember together what we read...

- Where did Jesus head to with His disciples? *Back alongside the sea.*

- Who followed after them as they went? *A huge crowd of people.*

- Where were some of the places we're told the people came from? *Galilee, from Judea, from Jerusalem, from Idumaea, beyond the Jordan, and those from around Tyre and Sidon.*

- Why did they come and follow Him? *Because they'd heard what "great things" He did.*

- Where was Jesus thinking He might need to sit, because the crowds were pressing so close? *In a boat out on the water.*

- Why did everyone press so close? *Because He healed so many and even His touch had so much power.*

- What did even the evil spirits shout out when they saw Jesus? *"You are the Son of God!"*

A question for us to ponder together...

1. When you imagine this whole scene—with the sea and the hills and the bright blue sky overhead, with the huge crowds of people all around, with Jesus sitting out in the boat teaching—what are some of your favorite little details to imagine?

Chapter 14

Jesus and the Twelve

Mark 3:13-19

¹³ *He went up into the mountain and called to himself those whom he wanted, and they went to him.* ¹⁴ *He appointed twelve, that they might be with him, and that he might send them out to preach* ¹⁵ *and to have authority to heal sicknesses and to cast out demons:* ¹⁶ *Simon (to whom he gave the name Peter);* ¹⁷ *James the son of Zebedee; and John, the brother of James, (whom he called Boanerges, which means, Sons of Thunder);* ¹⁸ *Andrew; Philip; Bartholomew; Matthew; Thomas; James, the son of Alphaeus; Thaddaeus; Simon the Zealot;* ¹⁹ *and Judas Iscariot, who also betrayed him.*

Let's remember together what we read...

- Where did Jesus go? *Up a mountain.*

- Who did He invite to come up there with Him? *His chosen friends.*

- How many disciples did He appoint to be His inner circle? *Twelve.*

- What are the specific assignments Mark mentions that these twelve were to be about? *Being with Jesus; being ready to be sent out to preach; having authority to heal and to cast out evil spirits.*

- How many of the Twelve can you name? *Simon Peter; James the son of Zebedee and John, the brother of James; Andrew; Philip; Bartholomew; Matthew; Thomas; James, the son of Alphaeus; Thaddaeus; Simon (called the Zealot); and Judas Iscariot.*

Questions for us to ponder together...

1. How do you think the Twelve felt about Jesus calling them into this special role?

2. How do you think *you* would feel if He'd called, or if He's calling you to something similar?

Chapter 15

Jesus versus Satan

Mark 3:19b-30

¹⁹ *Then he came into a house.* ²⁰ *The multitude came together again, so that they could not so much as eat bread.* ²¹ *When his friends heard it, they went out to seize him; for they said, "He is insane."* ²² *The scribes who came down from Jerusalem said, "He has Beelzebul," and, "By the prince of the demons he casts out the demons."*

²³ *He summoned them and said to them in parables, "How can Satan cast out Satan?* ²⁴ *If a kingdom is divided against itself, that kingdom cannot stand.* ²⁵ *If a house is divided against itself, that house cannot stand.* ²⁶ *If Satan has risen up against himself, and is divided, he can't stand, but has an end.* ²⁷ *But no one can enter into the house of the strong man to plunder unless he first binds the strong man; then he will plunder his house.*

²⁸ *"Most certainly I tell you, all sins of the descendants of man will be forgiven, including their blasphemies with which they may blaspheme;* ²⁹ *but whoever may blaspheme against the Holy Spirit never has forgiveness, but is subject to eternal condemnation."* ³⁰—*because they said, "He has an unclean spirit."*

Let's remember together what we read...

- Where did this whole conversation take place? *In someone's house.*

- How many people were there and nearby—a few or a lot? *A "multitude."*

- Did Jesus have a lot of "me time" during this whole season? *No! He could hardly get time and space to eat!*

- What did the intensity of His schedule make His own friends think? *That He'd lost His mind!*

- What terrible thought did the religious leaders have of Him? *That He was working with satan!*

- What did Jesus say to their accusation? *That, of course, satan can't cast out satan—that would make no sense! That only an **opposite** power can confront the evil one. That, in fact, He had come to break into satan's house, to tie him up, and to take back what belonged to God!*

- What, according to Jesus, is the single and only sin that God cannot forgive? *Blaspheming—talking falsely and in an unholy way—about the Holy Spirit.*

Questions for us to ponder together...

1. How does it make you feel to know that Jesus *isn't afraid at all* of the evil one, of evil, of anything at all?

2. How does seeing His power and courage encourage your own heart?

Chapter 16

Jesus and His New Heavenly Family

Mark 3:31-35

³¹ *His mother and his brothers came, and standing outside, they sent to him, calling him.* ³² *A multitude was sitting around him, and they told him, "Behold, your mother, your brothers, and your sisters are outside looking for you."*

³³ *He answered them, "Who are my mother and my brothers?"* ³⁴ *Looking around at those who sat around him, he said, "Behold, my mother and my brothers!* ³⁵ *For whoever does the will of God is my brother, my sister, and mother."*

Let's remember together what we read...

- Who came to visit Jesus in this moment? *His mother and His brothers (and, as we hear in a second, His sisters too).*

- Did they come into the house where He was staying? *No, they stood outside and sent for Him to come out to them.*

- At the time, how many people were hanging around Jesus? *Yet again, a "multitude."*

- What did the people tell Jesus? *"Your mother and brothers and sisters are outside looking for you."*

- Almost strangely, what question did Jesus ask in return? *"Who are my mother and my brothers?"*

- What did He do next? *Looked intently around Himself at those who were gathering there with Him.*

- And then what did He say? *"Here are my brothers and sisters! Whoever does the will of God is my family now!"*

Questions for us to ponder together...

1. How do you think Jesus' family felt when they heard His response to their coming?

2. How do *you* feel knowing that Jesus invites you to become part of the "inner circle" of His heavenly family?

Chapter 17

Jesus and the (First) Parable of the Sower

Mark 4:1-9

⁴ *Again he began to teach by the seaside. A great multitude was gathered to him, so that he entered into a boat in the sea, and sat down. All the multitude were on the land by the sea.* ² *He taught them many things in parables, and told them in his teaching,* ³ *"Listen! Behold, the farmer went out to sow,* ⁴ *and as he sowed, some seed fell by the road, and the birds came and devoured it.* ⁵ *Others fell on the rocky ground, where it had little soil, and immediately it sprang up, because it had no depth of soil.* ⁶ *When the sun had risen, it was scorched; and because it had no root, it withered away.* ⁷ *Others fell among the thorns, and the thorns grew up, and choked it, and it yielded no fruit.* ⁸ *Others fell into the good ground, and yielded fruit, growing up and increasing. Some produced thirty times, some sixty times, and some one hundred times as much."* ⁹ *He said, "Whoever has ears to hear, let him hear."*

Let's remember together what we read...

- Where did Jesus go to teach? *By the seaside.*

- Were there just a few folks gathered round Him, or a lot? *Yet again, a great "multitude."*

- Where did Jesus decide to sit while He taught them? *In a boat out on the water.*

- In Jesus' parable (which simply means a story with a special point), who was the main character? *A farmer.*

- And what was this farmer doing? *Sowing seed.*

- What happened to each of the seeds Jesus describes? *The first was immediately gobbled up by birds; the second fell on rocky ground which had shallow soil, so its roots were weak, and it died in the hot sunlight; the third fell among thorns and was choked by them; the final fell into good soil, grew strong, and produced good fruit.*

- How much good fruit did the fourth seed produce? *Thirty, sixty, even one hundred times as much as was sown.*

- What did Jesus say last to the crowds as a commandment to them? *"Whoever has ears to hear, let him hear."*

Questions for us to ponder together...

1. As we'll continue to see, Jesus loved to teach people with parables. Why do you think He did that?

2. If you had to explain the meaning of this "parable of the sower" to a friend, what would you say?

Chapter 18

Jesus and His Explanation of the (First) Parable of the Sower

Mark 4:10-20

¹⁰ *When he was alone, those who were around him with the twelve asked him about the parables.* ¹¹ *He said to them, "To you is given the mystery of God's Kingdom, but to those who are outside, all things are done in parables,* ¹² *that 'seeing they may see, and not perceive; and hearing they may hear, and not understand; lest perhaps they should turn again, and their sins should be forgiven them.'"*

¹³ *He said to them, "Don't you understand this parable? How will you understand all of the parables?* ¹⁴ *The farmer sows the word.* ¹⁵ *The ones by the road are the ones where the word is sown; and when they have heard, immediately Satan comes, and takes away the word which has been sown in them.* ¹⁶ *These in the same way are those who are sown on the rocky places, who, when they have heard the word, immediately receive it with joy.* ¹⁷ *They have no root in themselves, but are short-lived. When oppression or persecution arises because of the word, immediately they stumble.* ¹⁸ *Others are those who are sown among the thorns. These are those who have heard the word,* ¹⁹ *and the cares of this age, and the deceitfulness of riches, and the lusts of other things entering in choke the word, and it becomes unfruitful.*

²⁰ *Those which were sown on the good ground are those who hear the word, and accept it, and bear fruit, some thirty times, some sixty times, and some one hundred times."*

Let's remember together what we read...

- When did the Twelve ask Jesus about the "parable of the sower"? *When He was alone and away from the big crowds.*

- Before He explained the parable, what did Jesus say to the disciples about their opportunity in being near to Him? *That, being near Him, they are being "given the mystery of God's Kingdom."*

- Why does Jesus say that He speaks to the crowds with parables? *Because—using the words of the prophet Isaiah to explain—He wants to create spiritual mystery for those who are listening to Him. (Parent note: Remind your kids of how, when they hear something is "off limits" to them, it only increases their curiosity and desire to get near that thing. Jesus was well aware of how to draw even those folks who didn't initially seem interested!)*

- When Jesus starts explaining the parable, what does He say the "farmer" was sowing? *The "Word"—meaning, the Word of God.*

- What does He say happens to the first set of people who hear the Word? *Satan comes and steals it from their hearts and minds.*

- What does He say happens to the second? *They don't put down spiritual roots, so their faith is "short-lived."*

- What does He say happens to the third? *They are overwhelmed by the world around them—by worries, money, unclean living—and don't produce any fruit.*

- What does He say about the final people? *They hear the Word, "accept it," and bear a great amount of fruit.*

Questions for us to ponder together...

1. How does it feel to know that, knowing Jesus, we've *already been given* the secrets of the Kingdom of Heaven?

2. What does it mean to "accept" His words into our hearts?

Chapter 19

Jesus and the Parable of the Lamp

Mark 4:21-25

21 *He said to them, "Is the lamp brought to be put under a basket or under a bed? Isn't it put on a stand?* 22 *For there is nothing hidden, except that it should be made known; neither was anything made secret, but that it should come to light.* 23 *If any man has ears to hear, let him hear."*

24 *He said to them, "Take heed what you hear. With whatever measure you measure, it will be measured to you, and more will be given to you who hear.* 25 *For whoever has, to him more will be given, and he who doesn't have, even that which he has will be taken away from him."*

Let's remember together what we read...

- What item is at the center of this parable? *A lamp.*

- Where are the two places Jesus says you *wouldn't* probably put a lamp? *Under a basket or under a bed.*

- Where, instead, would you *want* to put a lamp? *Up on a lampstand.*

- What does Jesus tell us will happen to "hidden" things when the Kingdom comes? *They will be made known.*

- What about "secret" things? *They will come to light.*

- What does Jesus say about paying attention to what we hear? *We should be careful—or, as He says, "take heed."*

- Why should we be careful about what we hear—what we listen to? *Because according to the "measure" of what we're listening to, we'll have our lives' measured. (Parent note: Jesus wants us to understand the value of our ears—and, with that, our minds—and is teaching His disciples how to "give themselves" to things that truly matter, i.e. His living words.)*

- When we "have" some of Jesus' words, what does He say will happen in the future? *We will be given even more!*

- But if we ignore Jesus' words and don't possess them for ourselves, what does He say will happen? *We'll end up with nothing at all.*

Questions for us to ponder together...

1. What are the best ways to put Jesus' light up on the "lampstand" of your life?

2. What is a word of Jesus' that you've really taken to heart? What does it mean to you?

Chapter 20

Jesus and the (Second) Parable of a Sower

Mark 4:26-29

²⁶ *He said, "God's Kingdom is as if a man should cast seed on the earth,* ²⁷ *and should sleep and rise night and day, and the seed should spring up and grow, though he doesn't know how.* ²⁸ *For the earth bears fruit by itself: first the blade, then the ear, then the full grain in the ear.* ²⁹ *But when the fruit is ripe, immediately he puts in the sickle, because the harvest has come."*

Let's remember together what we read...

- As Jesus begins another parable, what does He tell us this one is like? *God's Kingdom.*

- What is the *action* He tells us is like the Kingdom of God? *Again, a man casting seed on the ground.*

- After this man sows seed, what does Jesus describe him doing? *Just going on with his life: sleeping, rising, living.*

- What happens to the seed while the man is going about his life? *It springs up and grows.*

- Does the man understand how the seed's springing up and growing works? *No!*

- Yet after the seed has fully grown, what does the man do? *Harvests it.*

- Why? *Because it's harvest time!*

Questions for us to ponder together...

1. What do you think Jesus means by this parable?

2. Does it bother Him if we don't always understand everything about the Kingdom of Heaven?

Chapter 21

Jesus and the Parable of the Mustard Seed

Mark 4:30-34

³⁰ He said, "How will we liken God's Kingdom? Or with what parable will we illustrate it? ³¹ It's like a grain of mustard seed, which, when it is sown in the earth, though it is less than all the seeds that are on the earth, ³² yet when it is sown, grows up, and becomes greater than all the herbs, and puts out great branches, so that the birds of the sky can lodge under its shadow."

³³ With many such parables he spoke the word to them, as they were able to hear it. ³⁴ Without a parable he didn't speak to them; but privately to his own disciples he explained everything.

Let's remember together what we read...

- In this next parable, what does Jesus say the Kingdom of God is like? *A mustard seed.*

- Where is the mustard seed placed? *In the ground.*

- Is it big or little? *It is one of the smallest of all seeds.*

- And yet what happens to it after it's sown in the ground? *It sprouts up, becomes bigger than practically any other herb, and grows great big branches, which even the birds of the sky like to come and hide in.*

- According to Mark, did Jesus often speak without using a parable? *No, He always used parables.*

- And who were the only ones to whom He explained their meaning? *His twelve disciples.*

Questions for us to ponder together...

1. So, according to this parable of the mustard seed, what does Jesus tell us the Kingdom of God is like?

2. What kind of people can Jesus use in His Kingdom—only "big, important people" or absolutely anyone, no matter their size or shape?

Chapter 22

Jesus Calms a Great Storm

Mark 4:35-41

³⁵ *On that day, when evening had come, he said to them, "Let's go over to the other side."* ³⁶ *Leaving the multitude, they took him with them, even as he was, in the boat. Other small boats were also with him.* ³⁷ *A big wind storm arose, and the waves beat into the boat, so much that the boat was already filled.* ³⁸ *He himself was in the stern, asleep on the cushion, and they woke him up, and told him, "Teacher, don't you care that we are dying?"*

³⁹ *He awoke, and rebuked the wind, and said to the sea, "Peace! Be still!" The wind ceased, and there was a great calm.* ⁴⁰ *He said to them, "Why are you so afraid? How is it that you have no faith?"*

⁴¹ *They were greatly afraid, and said to one another, "Who then is this, that even the wind and the sea obey him?"*

Let's remember together what we read...

- On what day did all of this happen? *On the very same day when He'd been speaking so many parables to the crowds by the seashore.*

- What time of day did this next adventure start? *Evening time.*

- What did Jesus say to His friends at the start? *"Let's go over to the other side" (of the Sea of Galilee).*

- Who went with Him? *Just His disciples—the crowds stayed behind.*

- How did He and His disciples travel? *By boat.*

- Were they entirely alone? *No, there were some other boats along with theirs.*

- Then, out there on the water, what began to happen? *A great big wind storm started.*

- What did the wind do to the waters of the sea? *Made them rise into waves and beat against the boat.*

- What did these waves do to Jesus' boat? *Started to fill it with water.*

- What was Jesus doing during this time? *Sleeping!*

- Where? *On a cushion in the stern (rear) of the boat.*

- In their fear, what did Jesus' disciples do? *Woke Him up, shouting, "Teacher, don't you care that we are dying?"*

- Did Jesus answer this question with words? *No.*

- Instead, what did He do? *"Rebuked" the wind and said to the sea, "Peace! Be still!"*

- And then what happened? *The wind stopped instantly; the sea's waves quieted to a great calm.*

- What did Jesus then say to His friends? *"Why are you so afraid? How is it that you have no faith?"*

- What emotion did the disciples feel after seeing all this? *Fear.*

- What did they ask themselves? *"Who is this—even the wind and the sea obey Him?!"*

Questions for us to ponder together...

1. When you imagine what happened on the waters that night, what is the part that most amazes or excites you?

2. What do we learn about Jesus—about His power, about His personality, about His relationship with His friends—when we read of the experience of that night?

Chapter 23

Jesus Sets "Legion" Free

Mark 5:1-20

[1] *They came to the other side of the sea, into the country of the Gadarenes.* [2] *When he had come out of the boat, immediately a man with an unclean spirit met him out of the tombs.* [3] *He lived in the tombs. Nobody could bind him any more, not even with chains,* [4] *because he had been often bound with fetters and chains, and the chains had been torn apart by him, and the fetters broken in pieces. Nobody had the strength to tame him.* [5] *Always, night and day, in the tombs and in the mountains, he was crying out, and cutting himself with stones.* [6] *When he saw Jesus from afar, he ran and bowed down to him,* [7] *and crying out with a loud voice, he said, "What have I to do with you, Jesus, you Son of the Most High God? I adjure you by God, don't torment me."* [8] *For he said to him, "Come out of the man, you unclean spirit!"*

[9] *He asked him, "What is your name?"*

He said to him, "My name is Legion, for we are many." [10] *He begged him much that he would not send them away out of the country.* [11] *Now on the mountainside there was a great herd of pigs feeding.* [12] *All the demons begged him, saying, "Send us into the pigs, that we may enter into them."*

[13] *At once Jesus gave them permission. The unclean spirits came out and entered into the pigs. The herd of about two thousand rushed down the steep bank into the sea,*

and they were drowned in the sea. ¹⁴ Those who fed the pigs fled, and told it in the city and in the country.

The people came to see what it was that had happened. ¹⁵ They came to Jesus, and saw him who had been possessed by demons sitting, clothed, and in his right mind, even him who had the legion; and they were afraid. ¹⁶ Those who saw it declared to them what happened to him who was possessed by demons, and about the pigs. ¹⁷ They began to beg him to depart from their region.

¹⁸ As he was entering into the boat, he who had been possessed by demons begged him that he might be with him. ¹⁹ He didn't allow him, but said to him, "Go to your house, to your friends, and tell them what great things the Lord has done for you, and how he had mercy on you."

²⁰ He went his way, and began to proclaim in Decapolis how Jesus had done great things for him, and everyone marveled.

Let's remember together what we read...

- On what day did this happen? *On the day after Jesus spoke many parables; after the night when Jesus calmed the storm.*

- Where did this happen? *On the other side of the Sea of Galilee (the eastern side), opposite where He did the majority of His ministry.*

- As Jesus and His disciples were getting out of their boat, who came running at them? *A demon-possessed man.*

- Where did this man live? Amidst the tombs—in a graveyard.

- What was his life like? *Terrible. People had often tried to chain him. Night and day, he screamed and cut himself.*

- What did this man do *first* when he saw Jesus? *Ran to Him and then bowed down to Him.*

- What did Jesus *first* say to the spirit within the man? *"Come out of this man, you unclean spirit!"*

- And what did the unclean spirit say back to Jesus? *"What have I to do with you, Jesus, you Son of the Most High God? By God I beg you, don't torture me!"*

- What did Jesus then ask? *The man's (or, really, the unclean spirit's) name.*

- And what was the answer? *"Legion," which was a unit in the Roman army that would've had thousands of men.*

- What did the unclean spirits then ask of Jesus? *To be cast out into a herd of pigs grazing nearby.*

- How many pigs are we told there were? *Nearly 2,000.*

- What happened when Jesus cast the "legion" of unclean spirits out of the man? *They dashed down into the sea and were all drowned.*

- Who, in fear, ran away to tell everyone what happened? *The keepers of the pigs.*

- When all the people came to see what had happened, how did they find the man who'd formerly lived in the graveyard? *Sitting there with Jesus, with his clothes on, perfectly normal.*

- What emotion did this cause in the people who saw him? *Fear.*

- What did these townspeople ask of Jesus? *For Him to leave immediately.*

- As Jesus was leaving, what did the formerly possessed man ask? *If he could go with Him wherever He was going.*

- What did Jesus tell him to do instead? *To go home to his friends and tell everyone, everywhere of what Jesus had done for him.*

- And what did the man do? *Exactly what Jesus asked of him.*

Questions for us to ponder together...

1. When you listen to the story of this day, how does it make you feel?

2. How do you imagine the look on Jesus' face during each part: when "Legion" first ran up; when the unclean spirits spoke; when He cast out the spirits; when the man asked to go with Him?

Chapter 24

Jesus, Jairus, and a Sick Woman: Part One

Mark 5:21-34

²¹ *When Jesus had crossed back over in the boat to the other side, a great multitude was gathered to him; and he was by the sea.* ²² *Behold, one of the rulers of the synagogue, Jairus by name, came; and seeing him, he fell at his feet,* ²³ *and begged him much, saying, "My little daughter is at the point of death. Please come and lay your hands on her, that she may be made healthy, and live."*

²⁴ *He went with him, and a great multitude followed him, and they pressed upon him on all sides.* ²⁵ *A certain woman, who had a discharge of blood for twelve years,* ²⁶ *and had suffered many things by many physicians, and had spent all that she had, and was no better, but rather grew worse,* ²⁷ *having heard the things concerning Jesus, came up behind him in the crowd, and touched his clothes.* ²⁸ *For she said, "If I just touch his clothes, I will be made well."* ²⁹ *Immediately the flow of her blood was dried up, and she felt in her body that she was healed of her affliction.*

³⁰ *Immediately Jesus, perceiving in himself that the power had gone out from him, turned around in the crowd, and asked, "Who touched my clothes?"*

³¹ *His disciples said to him, "You see the multitude pressing against you, and you say, 'Who touched me?'"*

³² *He looked around to see her who had done this thing.*
³³ *But the woman, fearing and trembling, knowing what had been done to her, came and fell down before him, and told him all the truth.*

³⁴ *He said to her, "Daughter, your faith has made you well. Go in peace, and be cured of your disease."*

TO BE CONTINUED...

Let's remember together what we read...

- Where did Jesus "cross back over in the boat" from? *The freeing of the man filled with a "legion" of demons.*

- Who was already waiting for Him before He'd even arrived? *A great multitude of people.*

- Who came right up to Him? *Jairus, one of the rulers of the synagogue.*

- What did Jairus do? *Fell down at Jesus' feet.*

- What did he beg Jesus to do? *To come to his house, to lay His hands upon his daughter—who was "at the point of death"—and to heal her.*

- Did Jesus take His time in answering this request? *No! He went immediately with Jairus.*

- How many people went along with Him on this healing errand? *The same great multitude, pressing all around Him.*

- Then who came toward Jesus? *A woman who was very sick with a condition of bleeding.*

- What are we told about her life's story? *That she'd had this condition for twelve years; that she had suffered because of many physician's treatments; that she was not getting better, only ever worse.*

- How did she approach Jesus? *Quietly, trying not to be noticed by Him or anyone else.*

- And what did she do? *Reached out and touched His clothes.*

- Why did she do this? *Because she believed He was so powerful that even just touching His clothes had the power to heal her.*

- Was she right? *Yes! The moment she touched Jesus, she was instantly healed of her whole twelve-year-long condition.*

- What did Jesus feel in that exact moment? *That power had gone out from Him into her.*

- And what did Jesus say in that moment? *"Who touched my clothes?"*

- How did Jesus' friends react to that question? *In essence, "Jesus, **everyone** is touching You!"*

- How did Jesus react to His friends' words? *He didn't answer—He continued looking around to spot the person who'd touched Him.*

- Then what did the woman who'd been healed do? *She came to Him, fell down at His feet, and told Him the whole story of her life, her sickness, and what she'd done in order to be healed by Him.*

- What did Jesus say in response? *"Daughter, your faith has made you well. Go in peace, and be cured of your disease."*

Questions for us to ponder together...

1. What do you learn about Jesus when you imagine this whole scene and all that happened?

2. How did that woman feel after her interaction with Jesus?

3. How do you think Jairus was feeling while he stood there and watched that interaction?

Chapter 25

Jesus, Jairus, and a Sick Woman: Part Two

Mark 5:35-43

³⁵ *While he was still speaking [to the woman healed of her bleeding condition], people came from the synagogue ruler's house saying, "Your daughter is dead. Why bother the Teacher any more?"*

³⁶ *But Jesus, when he heard the message spoken, immediately said to the ruler of the synagogue, "Don't be afraid, only believe."* ³⁷ *He allowed no one to follow him, except Peter, James, and John the brother of James.* ³⁸ *He came to the synagogue ruler's house, and he saw an uproar, weeping, and great wailing.* ³⁹ *When he had entered in, he said to them, "Why do you make an uproar and weep? The child is not dead, but is asleep."*

⁴⁰ *They ridiculed him. But he, having put them all out, took the father of the child, her mother, and those who were with him, and went in where the child was lying.* ⁴¹ *Taking the child by the hand, he said to her, "Talitha cumi!" which means, being interpreted, "Girl, I tell you, get up!"* ⁴² *Immediately the girl rose up and walked, for she was twelve years old. They were amazed with great amazement.* ⁴³ *He strictly ordered them that no one should know this, and commanded that something should be given to her to eat.*

Let's remember together what we read...

- Who is Jesus talking to at the beginning of our continued account? *The woman who He'd just healed of her bleeding condition.*

- Who then arrived on the scene? *People from the house of Jairus, the synagogue ruler.*

- What did they tell Jairus? *That his daughter has died; that he need not bother Jesus anymore.*

- What did Jesus say to Jairus when He heard these people and their message? *"Don't be afraid, only believe."*

- Who did Jesus bring with Him as He then went with Jairus to his house? *Peter, James, and John.*

- What did they all see when they arrived at Jairus' house? *Everyone weeping and wailing and crying.*

- What did Jesus say to all these sad people? *"Why do you make all this noise? The child isn't dead—she's asleep."*

- How did all the people react? *They mocked Jesus' words.*

- Where did Jesus then go? *In where the little girl was lying.*

- What did Jesus do and say? *Took her hand and said to her, "Girl, get up!"*

- And what happened? *The little girl came back from the dead—she got up!*

- How old was she? *Twelve years old.*

- How did her parents and everyone who saw her alive react? *They were "amazed with great amazement."*

Questions for us to ponder together...

1. If you'd been Peter, James, or John invited to go with Jesus to Jairus' house, what do you think you'd have been feeling *before* the miracle occurred?

2. If you'd been Peter, James, or John invited to go with Jesus to Jairus' house, what do you think you'd have been feeling *after* the miracle occurred?

Chapter 26

Jesus in His Hometown

Mark 6:1-6

¹ *He went out from there. He came into his own country, and his disciples followed him.* ² *When the Sabbath had come, he began to teach in the synagogue, and many hearing him were astonished, saying, "Where did this man get these things?" and, "What is the wisdom that is given to this man, that such mighty works come about by his hands?* ³ *Isn't this the carpenter, the son of Mary, and brother of James, Joses, Judah, and Simon? Aren't his sisters here with us?" So they were offended at him.*

⁴ *Jesus said to them, "A prophet is not without honor, except in his own country, and among his own relatives, and in his own house."* ⁵ *He could do no mighty work there, except that he laid his hands on a few sick people, and healed them.* ⁶ *He marveled because of their unbelief.*

Let's remember together what we read...

- Where did Jesus go in this account? *Back to "his own country"—His hometown, Nazareth.*

- Who went with Him there? *His disciples.*

- On what day did this happen? *On the Sabbath.*

- What did Jesus do on that particular Sabbath? *Went into the synagogue of His hometown and began to teach.*

- How did the people of His hometown react? *They were astonished.*

- What did they say to each other? *"Where did He get all these teachings?" and "Where did He get all this wisdom and all this power?" and "Isn't this the guy who used to be our village carpenter and whose family we know?"*

- How did the townspeople end up feeling about Jesus? *Offended.*

- What did Jesus say to them? *"A prophet is honored except where he grew up."*

- And what, we are told, was the result upon Jesus' ministry in Nazareth? *He wasn't able to do many miracles there because of their unbelief.*

Questions for us to ponder together...

1. Why did the people of Nazareth react to Jesus in the way they did?

2. How do you think Jesus felt at the end of this day?

Chapter 27

Jesus Sends Out the Twelve

Mark 6:6b-13

⁶ *He went around the villages teaching.* ⁷ *He called to himself the twelve, and began to send them out two by two; and he gave them authority over the unclean spirits.* ⁸ *He commanded them that they should take nothing for their journey, except a staff only: no bread, no wallet, no money in their purse,* ⁹ *but to wear sandals, and not put on two tunics.* ¹⁰ *He said to them, "Wherever you enter into a house, stay there until you depart from there.* ¹¹ *Whoever will not receive you nor hear you, as you depart from there, shake off the dust that is under your feet for a testimony against them. Assuredly, I tell you, it will be more tolerable for Sodom and Gomorrah in the day of judgment than for that city!"*

¹² *They went out and preached that people should repent.* ¹³ *They cast out many demons, and anointed many with oil who were sick, and healed them.*

Let's remember together what we read...

- Where was Jesus doing His teaching? *Around all the villages surrounding the Sea of Galilee.*

- Who did He call near to have a talk? *The Twelve.*

- What was He preparing to do with them? *To send them out in His name.*

- How did He choose to send them out? *In pairs, "two by two."*

- Who did He give them "authority over"? *Unclean, evil spirits.*

- What were they to take with them? *Nothing except a staff for walking—no bread, no wallet, no extra money, just their sandals and one tunic.*

- Where were they supposed to stay in each town they came to? *The first house they were invited to stay at.*

- If they weren't accepted by townspeople, what were they supposed to do on their way out of town? *Shake off the dust of that town's streets from their feet. (Parent note: Beyond Jesus' words about judgment, this also meant that they weren't to let it bother them that they weren't accepted in a certain place; it was like our modern saying of "Brush it off," i.e. don't let it get under your skin.)*

- Was it a good thing for a town to receive that dusty "shake off"? *No! It meant that they were really rejecting God, just like the Old Testament towns of Sodom and Gomorrah.*

- What did the disciples preach when they went out? *That people should "repent," i.e. change their minds, hearts, and actions and move in the Way of Jesus.*

- What did the disciples do during their travels? *Cast out demons, anoint the sick with oil, and heal them.*

Questions for us to ponder together...

1. Why do you think Jesus sent out His friends without going with them?

2. Why do you think He sent them out with nothing but the clothes on their back?

3. What do you think those two-by-two travels did for the hearts of the Twelve?

Chapter 28

What Happened to Jesus' Cousin, John the Baptist

Mark 6:14-29

[14] *King Herod heard [about the disciples of Jesus traveling and healing people in His name], for his name had become known, and he said, "John the Baptizer has risen from the dead, and therefore these powers are at work in him."* [15] *But others said, "He is Elijah." Others said, "He is a prophet, or like one of the prophets."* [16] *But Herod, when he heard this, said, "This is John, whom I beheaded. He has risen from the dead."* [17] *For Herod himself had sent out and arrested John, and bound him in prison for the sake of Herodias, his brother Philip's wife, for he had married her.* [18] *For John said to Herod, "It is not lawful for you to have your brother's wife."* [19] *Herodias set herself against him, and desired to kill him, but she couldn't,* [20] *for Herod feared John, knowing that he was a righteous and holy man, and kept him safe. When he heard him, he did many things, and he heard him gladly.*

[21] *Then a convenient day came, that Herod on his birthday made a supper for his nobles, the high officers, and the chief men of Galilee.* [22] *When the daughter of Herodias herself came in and danced, she pleased Herod and those sitting with him. The king said to the young lady, "Ask me whatever you want, and I will give it to you."*

²³ He swore to her, "Whatever you shall ask of me, I will give you, up to half of my kingdom."

²⁴ She went out, and said to her mother, "What shall I ask?" She said, "The head of John the Baptizer."

²⁵ She came in immediately with haste to the king, and asked, "I want you to give me right now the head of John the Baptizer on a platter."

²⁶ The king was exceedingly sorry, but for the sake of his oaths, and of his dinner guests, he didn't wish to refuse her. ²⁷ Immediately the king sent out a soldier of his guard, and commanded to bring John's head, and he went and beheaded him in the prison, ²⁸ and brought his head on a platter, and gave it to the young lady; and the young lady gave it to her mother.

²⁹ When his disciples heard this, they came and took up his corpse, and laid it in a tomb.

Let's remember together what we read...

- Who heard about the disciples' traveling, preaching, and healing? *King Herod.*

- Who did Herod think Jesus perhaps was? *John the Baptist, back from the dead.*

- Why did Herod think that? *Because the miracles of Jesus told him that something truly supernatural was happening.*

- Why had Herod arrested John the Baptist in the first place? *Because John had told him that it wasn't right to have stolen his own brother's wife.*

- How did Herodias (Herod's new wife) feel about John the Baptist? *She hated him and wanted him dead.*

- How did Herod himself feel about John the Baptist? *He "feared" him, because he was righteous and set apart by God; plus, he was fascinated by his words and actions while he was in prison.*

- On what day was John the Baptist destined to die? *King Herod's birthday.*

- Who was assembled for the big birthday feast? *All the important people in the whole surrounding district.*

- Who came in to entertain all the noble people with a dance? *Herodias' daughter—who was Herod's step-daughter.*

- What foolish promise did Herod make to this young woman? *That she could ask for anything—up to half his kingdom—and it was hers.*

- Who did the young woman go talk to? *Her mother, Herodias.*

- And what did she then ask King Herod for? *John the Baptist's head on a platter.*

- Why couldn't King Herod say "no" to this terrible request? *Because, as king, he had given his royal word—and because there were people there who had witnessed the whole thing.*

- So what happened? *John the Baptist was beheaded (his head was cut off with a sword) and, like the young woman requested, his head was brought into the party on a royal platter.*

- Who then came to collect John the Baptist's body? *His own disciples, who had been with him ever since the baptisms out at the Jordan River.*

Questions for us to ponder together...

1. Knowing what we know about John the Baptist, what do you think was the purpose of his life?

2. Do you think John regretted dying for the sake of Jesus and His Kingdom?

Chapter 29

Jesus Miraculously Feeds a Great Crowd

Mark 6:30-44

³⁰ *The apostles gathered themselves together to Jesus, and they told him all things, whatever they had done, and whatever they had taught.* ³¹ *He said to them, "You come apart into a deserted place, and rest awhile." For there were many coming and going, and they had no leisure so much as to eat.* ³² *They went away in the boat to a deserted place by themselves.* ³³ *They saw them going, and many recognized him and ran there on foot from all the cities. They arrived before them and came together to him.* ³⁴ *Jesus came out, saw a great multitude, and he had compassion on them, because they were like sheep without a shepherd, and he began to teach them many things.* ³⁵ *When it was late in the day, his disciples came to him, and said, "This place is deserted, and it is late in the day.* ³⁶ *Send them away, that they may go into the surrounding country and villages, and buy themselves bread, for they have nothing to eat."*

³⁷ *But he answered them, "You give them something to eat."*

They asked him, "Shall we go and buy two hundred denarii worth of bread, and give them something to eat?"
³⁸ *He said to them, "How many loaves do you have? Go see."*

When they knew, they said, "Five, and two fish."

[39] He commanded them that everyone should sit down in groups on the green grass. [40] They sat down in ranks, by hundreds and by fifties. [41] He took the five loaves and the two fish, and looking up to heaven, he blessed and broke the loaves, and he gave to his disciples to set before them, and he divided the two fish among them all. [42] They all ate, and were filled. [43] They took up twelve baskets full of broken pieces and also of the fish. [44] Those who ate the loaves were five thousand men.

Let's remember together what we read...

- Who returned to Jesus at the beginning of this narrative? *The Twelve, fresh from their two-by-two traveling and preaching.*

- What did Jesus say in response to all their great stories of what happened? *"Let's go away and rest by ourselves for a while."*

- Where did Jesus and the Twelve then go? *Off to a deserted place in their own boat.*

- But who followed them? *A great big crowd of people. (They even got to where Jesus was going before **He** got there!)*

- How did Jesus feel when He got out of the boat and saw them all there? *Filled with compassion, "because they were like sheep without a shepherd."*

- So what did He do? *He began to teach them.*

- Later on, what was the disciples' advice to Jesus? *"It's getting late, Jesus. Let's let the crowds leave so that they may go get some dinner."*

- What did Jesus say back to His friends? *"You give them something to eat!"*

- Did His disciples immediately say "yes" to His request? *No, they were slightly amazed and skeptical at what He said.*

- What did Jesus then ask them to do? *Go out into the crowds and see how much food they could find.*

- And how much did they find? *Only five loaves of bread and two fish.*

- What did Jesus have the crowds do? *Take a seat in the grass in groups of 50 and 100.*

- Then what did He do? *Gave thanks for the food, started breaking it up and handing it to the disciples to hand out to the people.*

- How many people got food? *5,000 men, which doesn't even include all the women and children. (Parent note: There may have been double or even triple the 5,000 stated!)*

- Did everyone get enough food? *Yes! In fact, they were "satisfied"—meaning, really full!*

- Were there any leftovers? *Yes! Twelve whole basketfuls that were picked up by the **twelve** disciples!*

Questions for us to ponder together...

1. How do you think the disciples' view of Jesus changed from the beginning of that day to its end?

2. What do you like about Jesus' personality during this miraculous moment?

Chapter 30

Jesus Walks Atop the Sea of Galilee

Mark 6:45-52

⁴⁵ *Immediately he made his disciples get into the boat, and go ahead to the other side, to Bethsaida, while he himself sent the multitude away.* ⁴⁶ *After he had taken leave of them, he went up the mountain to pray.*

⁴⁷ *When evening had come, the boat was in the middle of the sea, and he was alone on the land.* ⁴⁸ *Seeing them distressed in rowing, for the wind was contrary to them, about the fourth watch of the night he came to them, walking on the sea, and he would have passed by them,* ⁴⁹ *but they, when they saw him walking on the sea, supposed that it was a ghost, and cried out;* ⁵⁰ *for they all saw him, and were troubled. But he immediately spoke with them, and said to them, "Cheer up! It is I! Don't be afraid."* ⁵¹ *He got into the boat with them; and the wind ceased, and they were very amazed among themselves, and marveled;* ⁵² *for they hadn't understood about the loaves, but their hearts were hardened.*

Let's remember together what we read...

- When does this narrative begin? *"Immediately" after Jesus had just fed the 5,000.*

- Where does Jesus send His friends? *Away in their boat, to go to the other side of the Sea, to the town of Bethsaida.*

- What was Jesus staying behind to do? *To personally send the great crowds on their way.*

- Then what did Jesus do? *Went farther up the mountain to spend time talking with His Father.*

- By the time darkness dropped, where were the disciples and Jesus? *The disciples were in the middle of the Sea and Jesus was still up on that mountain.*

- What were the disciples doing right then? *Rowing with all their might, because the wind was up and causing the Sea to be stormy.*

- Could Jesus see them out there? *Yes. (Parent note: Only Mark's Gospel specifically states that Jesus could see them out on the water—a very picturesque detail. Perhaps the moon was particularly strong that night.)*

- Then what did Jesus do? *He got up from praying, walked down the mountainside, and then (oh, so amazingly!) simply walked right out to them on the top of the wild waves!*

- When the disciples saw Him, what did they think? *They thought He was a ghost and screamed!*

- How did Jesus respond to their fear? *He said, "Cheer up! It's me! Don't be afraid."*

- Then what did He do? *Got right into the boat.*

- And then what happened? *All the wind suddenly stopped.*

- How did the disciples feel right then? *Amazed and a little bit overwhelmed. As Mark says, they simply hadn't understood the miracle of the 5,000—so everything keeps surprising them.*

Questions for us to ponder together...

1. Is there *anything in the whole wide world* that is impossible for Jesus?

2. What's your favorite thing to imagine about Jesus walking on the waters of the Sea of Galilee?

Chapter 31

Jesus' Healing Power Heals Everyone

Mark 6:53-56

53 *When they had crossed over, they came to land at Gennesaret, and moored to the shore.* 54 *When they had come out of the boat, immediately the people recognized him,* 55 *and ran around that whole region, and began to bring those who were sick on their mats to where they heard he was.* 56 *Wherever he entered, into villages, or into cities, or into the country, they laid the sick in the marketplaces, and begged him that they might just touch the fringe of his garment; and as many as touched him were made well.*

Let's remember together what we read...

- What were Jesus and His friends arriving to this shore from? *From the night when He'd walked on water and from the day before when He'd fed the enormous crowd with five loaves and two fish.*

- Where did they land? *Gennesaret.*

- What did the people of that district do? *When they recognized Jesus, they ran around the whole region and brought everyone who was sick to be healed by Him.*

- What happened in every place Jesus came to? *People laid their sick in His path, and they begged that they might even "just touch the fringe of his garment"—just like the bleeding woman had done before.*

- Who was healed by Jesus? *Everyone who touched Him!*

Questions for us to ponder together...

1. What do you think made Jesus so attractive to people?

2. Who are the people in your life who you'd like to get nearer to Jesus?

Chapter 32

A Confrontation with the Religious Leaders

Mark 7:1-13

¹ *Then the Pharisees and some of the scribes gathered together to him, having come from Jerusalem.* ² *Now when they saw some of his disciples eating bread with defiled, that is unwashed, hands, they found fault.* ³ *(For the Pharisees and all the Jews don't eat unless they wash their hands and forearms, holding to the tradition of the elders.* ⁴ *They don't eat when they come from the marketplace unless they bathe themselves, and there are many other things, which they have received to hold to: washings of cups, pitchers, bronze vessels, and couches.)* ⁵ *The Pharisees and the scribes asked him, "Why don't your disciples walk according to the tradition of the elders, but eat their bread with unwashed hands?"*

⁶ *He answered them, "Well did Isaiah prophesy of you hypocrites, as it is written,*

'This people honors me with their lips,
but their heart is far from me.
⁷ *But they worship me in vain,*
teaching as doctrines the commandments of men.'

⁸ *"For you set aside the commandment of God, and hold tightly to the tradition of men—the washing of pitchers and cups, and you do many other such things."* ⁹ *He said to them, "Full well do you reject the commandment of*

God, that you may keep your tradition. [10] For Moses said, 'Honor your father and your mother;' and, 'He who speaks evil of father or mother, let him be put to death.' [11] But you say, 'If a man tells his father or his mother, "Whatever profit you might have received from me is Corban,"'" that is to say, given to God, [12] "then you no longer allow him to do anything for his father or his mother, [13] making void the word of God by your tradition which you have handed down. You do many things like this."

Let's remember together what we read...

- Who "gathered" around Jesus at the beginning? *Some of the scribes and Pharisees.*

- Where had they come from to see Him? *Jerusalem, the capital city.*

- What did they quickly get upset about? *Some of Jesus' disciples eating their bread with unwashed hands.*

- Why did this bother them so much? *Because they themselves followed all kinds of special rules about washings, etc.*

- What did these scribes and Pharisees accuse His friends of not following? *The "tradition of the elders"— meaning, the passed-down-through-time teachings of the Jewish religious leaders throughout history.*

- Was Jesus pleased with their question and the heart behind it? *No! He said, like Isaiah had prophesied, that they only gave "lip service" and that they weren't following the true Way of God.*

- Which of the Ten Commandments does Jesus give as an example of a command they were breaking? *"Honor your father and your mother," which is the fifth commandment.*

- Why was Jesus so upset with the lifestyle and example of the scribes and Pharisees? *Because, in their concern for their own man-made traditions, they were completely ignoring what God actually said to them. **And**, because they were leaders in that culture, they were leading other people away from simply following God.*

Questions for us to ponder together...

1. Why do you think the religious leaders of Jesus' day didn't like Him?

2. What did Jesus want those religious leaders, themselves, to do?

Chapter 33

Jesus Talks About the Outside versus the Inside

Mark 7:14-23

¹⁴ *He called all the multitude to himself, and said to them, "Hear me, all of you, and understand.* ¹⁵ *There is nothing from outside of the man, that going into him can defile him; but the things which proceed out of the man are those that defile the man.* ¹⁶ *If anyone has ears to hear, let him hear!"*

¹⁷ *When he had entered into a house away from the multitude, his disciples asked him about the parable.* ¹⁸ *He said to them, "Are you also without understanding? Don't you perceive that whatever goes into the man from outside can't defile him,* ¹⁹ *because it doesn't go into his heart, but into his stomach, then into the latrine, making all foods clean?"* ²⁰ *He said, "That which proceeds out of the man, that defiles the man.* ²¹ *For from within, out of the hearts of men, proceed evil thoughts, adulteries, sexual sins, murders, thefts,* ²² *covetings, wickedness, deceit, lustful desires, an evil eye, blasphemy, pride, and foolishness.* ²³ *All these evil things come from within, and defile the man."*

Let's remember together what we read...

- Who did Jesus call near to Him after His argument with the scribes and Pharisees? *All the people of the great multitude.*

- What did He teach the people of the great crowd? *That no food or unclean surface could hurt a person's inner life; that it was a person's inner life that actually decided what their "outer self" was like.*

- Where did Jesus go after He said these things? *Into someone's house, away from the bigger crowds of people.*

- What did the disciples ask Jesus? *To explain what He'd said to the crowds outside.*

- How did Jesus explain His earlier words? *That food (or food eaten with "unclean hands") doesn't ruin a person's inner life because it's simply eaten, digested, and then passed. It is an "unclean heart"—filled with evil thoughts, unkind ideas, pride, etc.—that is actually the problem. The wrong kind of heart is the sin, not the wrong kind of food.*

Questions for us to ponder together...

1. Why was it so important for Jesus to clear up this religious misunderstanding?

2. What was (and is) Jesus wanting to do in our inmost hearts?

Chapter 34

Jesus Meets a Desperate Mother

Mark 7:24-30

[24] *From there he arose, and went away into the borders of Tyre and Sidon. He entered into a house, and didn't want anyone to know it, but he couldn't escape notice.* [25] *For a woman, whose little daughter had an unclean spirit, having heard of him, came and fell down at his feet.* [26] *Now the woman was a Greek, a Syrophoenician by race. She begged him that he would cast the demon out of her daughter.* [27] *But Jesus said to her, "Let the children be filled first, for it is not appropriate to take the children's bread and throw it to the dogs."*

[28] *But she answered him, "Yes, Lord. Yet even the dogs under the table eat the children's crumbs."*

[29] *He said to her, "For this saying, go your way. The demon has gone out of your daughter."*

[30] *She went away to her house, and found the child having been laid on the bed, with the demon gone out.*

Let's remember together what we read...

- Where did Jesus travel to? *The borderland of Tyre and Sidon.*

- Once there, where did He go? *Into someone's house.*

- Why? *Because He wanted to **not** be noticed by the crowds of people.*

- Did He avoid being noticed? *No, the woman in this account heard about Him and came immediately to Him.*

- What did she do the minute she saw Jesus? *Fell down at His feet.*

- Why had she come to Him? *Because her daughter had an unclean spirit.*

- Was this mother a member of the people of Israel? *No, she was a "Greek" (or a Gentile—meaning, a non-Jewish person).*

- What were the strange words that Jesus spoke to test this woman's faith? *"Let the children be filled first, for it is not appropriate to take the children's bread and throw it to the dogs."*

- How—and quite boldly!—did the mother answer Jesus' strange words? *"Yes, Lord. Yet even the dogs under the table eat the children's crumbs."*

- What did Jesus do in response to her boldness? *Immediately set her daughter free—even though she was at a distance!*

- What did the mother find when she got home? *That her daughter was totally well—back to normal.*

Questions for us to ponder together...

1. Why do you think Jesus spoke such seemingly harsh words to this worried mother?

2. What do you think she received from Him, even beyond the healing of her daughter?

Chapter 35

Jesus Heals a Man Who Can't Hear or Speak

Mark 7:31-37

³¹ *Again he departed from the borders of Tyre and Sidon, and came to the sea of Galilee, through the middle of the region of Decapolis.* ³² *They brought to him one who was deaf and had an impediment in his speech. They begged him to lay his hand on him.* ³³ *He took him aside from the multitude, privately, and put his fingers into his ears, and he spat, and touched his tongue.* ³⁴ *Looking up to heaven, he sighed, and said to him, "Ephphatha!" that is, "Be opened!"* ³⁵ *Immediately his ears were opened, and the impediment of his tongue was released, and he spoke clearly.* ³⁶ *He commanded them that they should tell no one, but the more he commanded them, so much the more widely they proclaimed it.* ³⁷ *They were astonished beyond measure, saying, "He has done all things well. He makes even the deaf hear, and the mute speak!"*

Let's remember together what we read...

- Where did Jesus travel away from? *From the borders of Tyre and Sidon, where He'd healed the daughter of the woman who came to Him.*

- Where did He return to? *Back to the Sea of Galilee.*

- And what region did He pass through to get there? *The Decapolis. (Parent note: This simply means "The Ten Towns"—a region known for the ten towns that comprised it.)*

- Who was brought to Jesus—and why? *A man who couldn't hear and who also couldn't speak; the people wanted Jesus to heal him.*

- Where did Jesus take this man? *Away from the big crowds so they could be alone.*

- What did Jesus do to the man? *Put his fingers into the man's ears, then spat, then touched his tongue.*

- Then what did Jesus do? *Looked up to Heaven, sighed, and said "Be opened!"*

- What happened to the man? *He could hear! He could speak!*

- What did Jesus tell the people who saw this? *That they shouldn't tell anyone.*

- And yet, what did they do? *Told everyone!*

- What did they tell everyone? *That Jesus did everything well—and that He could even heal the deaf and those who couldn't speak!*

Questions for us to ponder together...

1. Imagine if you yourself couldn't hear or speak. Describe how you would feel—what you would notice, be excited about, be amazed by—if suddenly Jesus healed you!

2. What do you think this man's first reaction was?

Chapter 36

Jesus (*Again!*) Miraculously Feeds a Great Crowd

Mark 8:1-9

¹ *In those days, when there was a very great multitude, and they had nothing to eat, Jesus called his disciples to himself, and said to them,* ² *"I have compassion on the multitude, because they have stayed with me now three days, and have nothing to eat.* ³ *If I send them away fasting to their home, they will faint on the way, for some of them have come a long way."*

⁴ *His disciples answered him, "From where could one satisfy these people with bread here in a deserted place?"*

⁵ *He asked them, "How many loaves do you have?"*

They said, "Seven."

⁶ *He commanded the multitude to sit down on the ground, and he took the seven loaves. Having given thanks, he broke them, and gave them to his disciples to serve, and they served the multitude.* ⁷ *They had a few small fish. Having blessed them, he said to serve these also.* ⁸ *They ate, and were filled. They took up seven baskets of broken pieces that were left over.* ⁹ *Those who had eaten were about four thousand. Then he sent them away.*

Let's remember together what we read...

- How many people were gathered around Jesus? *Again, a "very great multitude."*

- When He saw that the people had nothing to eat, who did Jesus call near for a private conversation? *His disciples.*

- As you listen to what Jesus said to His friends ("I have compassion on the multitude, because they have stayed with me now three days, and have nothing to eat. If I send them away fasting to their home, they will faint on the way, for some of them have come a long way"), do His words remind you of anything we've heard before? *What He says to His disciples here sounds **very much** like what they'd said **to Him** before the "Feeding of the 5,000"!*

- Did the disciples pick up on that hint? *No! They imme-diately questioned whether anything was possible, given the situation!*

- What did Jesus ask them? *How many loaves they had.*

- How many loaves did they have? *Seven.*

- What did Jesus then do? *Everything He'd also done the first time He fed a huge crowd: had everyone sit down, gave thanks for the food, broke it, and handed it to the disciples to give to the people.*

- How many were miraculously fed on this day? *About 4,000. (Parent note: Most likely, this was again just a count of the men present. So there may have been 8,000 or 10,000 or 12,000 when accounting for women and children.)*

- Did they get enough? *Yes! In fact, they were "filled."*

- Were there any leftovers? *Yes! Seven basketfuls.*

Questions for us to ponder together...

1. Why do you think the disciples of Jesus didn't notice the similarities between the beginnings of this day and the day of the "Feeding of the 5,000"?

2. How will we learn to be good rememberers of all the Lord has done for us so that we're able to trust Him in every present moment?

Chapter 37

Jesus and the "Yeast" of the Religious Leaders

Mark 8:10-21

¹⁰ *Immediately he entered into the boat with his disciples, and came into the region of Dalmanutha.* ¹¹ *The Pharisees came out and began to question him, seeking from him a sign from heaven, and testing him.* ¹² *He sighed deeply in his spirit, and said, "Why does this generation seek a sign? Most certainly I tell you, no sign will be given to this generation."*

¹³ *He left them, and again entering into the boat, departed to the other side.* ¹⁴ *They forgot to take bread; and they didn't have more than one loaf in the boat with them.* ¹⁵ *He warned them, saying, "Take heed: beware of the yeast of the Pharisees and the yeast of Herod."*

¹⁶ *They reasoned with one another, saying, "It's because we have no bread."*

¹⁷ *Jesus, perceiving it, said to them, "Why do you reason that it's because you have no bread? Don't you perceive yet, neither understand? Is your heart still hardened?* ¹⁸ *Having eyes, don't you see? Having ears, don't you hear? Don't you remember?* ¹⁹ *When I broke the five loaves among the five thousand, how many baskets full of broken pieces did you take up?"*

They told him, "Twelve."

[20] *"When the seven loaves fed the four thousand, how many baskets full of broken pieces did you take up?"*

They told him, "Seven."

[21] *He asked them, "Don't you understand yet?"*

Let's remember together what we read...

- Where was Jesus leaving "immediately" from in the boat? *From His second miraculous feeding—this time, of 4,000.*

- Where did He arrive to? *The region of Dalmanutha.*

- Who came out to question Him? *The Pharisees.*

- What did they want from Jesus? *A "sign from heaven."*

- How did Jesus respond to this request? *He was frustrated and sighed. Then He said that He would **not** give a sign of the kind they were wanting.*

- After He and His disciples departed again across the Sea, what did the disciples happen to notice? *That they only had one loaf of bread for all of them to eat.*

- What warning did Jesus then speak to them? *"Beware of the yeast of the Pharisees and of Herod."*

- What did Jesus' friends think He was talking about? *The fact that they had no actual bread.*

- What did Jesus then ask them? *If they were paying attention **at all**! If their hearts, eyes, and ears were open **at all**!*

- What did He then ask them if they remembered? *How many basketfuls of leftovers were picked up after the two miraculous feedings.*

- Did they remember? *Yes—twelve and seven.*

- And what was Jesus' final question to them? *"Don't you understand yet?"*

Questions for us to ponder together...

1. Why did Jesus refuse to show a "sign from heaven" for the Pharisees?

2. Why do you think it mattered so much to Jesus that His disciples would "remember" and "understand" the miracles He was doing?

Chapter 38

Jesus Heals a Blind Man in Bethsaida

Mark 8:22-26

²² *He came to Bethsaida. They brought a blind man to him, and begged him to touch him.* ²³ *He took hold of the blind man by the hand, and brought him out of the village. When he had spat on his eyes, and laid his hands on him, he asked him if he saw anything.*

²⁴ *He looked up, and said, "I see men; for I see them like trees walking."*

²⁵ *Then again he laid his hands on his eyes. He looked intently, and was restored, and saw everyone clearly.* ²⁶ *He sent him away to his house, saying, "Don't enter into the village, nor tell anyone in the village."*

Let's remember together what we read...

- What was the name of the town where this happened? *Bethsaida.*

- Who was brought to Jesus by the townspeople? *A blind man.*

- Where did Jesus take the blind man "by the hand"? *Outside of the village—probably where fewer people would see what happened.*

- Then what did Jesus do? *He spat(!) on the man's eyes, put His hands upon him, and then asked what he could see.*

- What did the blind man see when he opened his eyes? *People—but in a blurry way, because they looked to him like trees walking around.*

- So what did Jesus do, next? *Laid His hands on him again.*

- And what did the man see now? *Everything and everyone clearly!*

- What did Jesus command the man? *"Stay out of the village and don't tell anyone."*

Questions for us to ponder together...

1. What does it teach us about Jesus that He wouldn't accept a "partial healing"?

2. If you'd never seen before, what do you think would be the most amazing thing about suddenly receiving your sight?

Chapter 39

"Who Do Men Say That I Am?"

Mark 8:27-30

[27] *Jesus went out, with his disciples, into the villages of Caesarea Philippi. On the way he asked his disciples, "Who do men say that I am?"*

[28] *They told him, "John the Baptizer, and others say Elijah, but others, one of the prophets."*

[29] *He said to them, "But who do you say that I am?" Peter answered, "You are the Christ."*

[30] *He commanded them that they should tell no one about him.*

Let's remember together what we read...

- Where was Jesus traveling to? *The villages of Caesarea Philippi. (Parent note: This is a region about 25 miles north of the Sea of Galilee known for its inclusion of worship of the Greek pantheon—especially the god Pan.)*

- What question did Jesus ask His friends while they walked? *"Who do men say that I am?"*

- What were the three answers His friends gave Him? *John the Baptist, the prophet Elijah, or another of the other Old Testament prophets.*

- Then what question did Jesus ask them? *"But who do **you** say that I am?"*

- Who was the disciple who answered for himself? *Peter.*

- What did Peter say? *"You are the Christ." (Parent note: "Christ" means "the Anointed One," which is another way of saying "Messiah"—the One all Israel had been waiting for.)*

- How did Jesus respond to Peter's confession of belief? *By telling them all to keep what they knew to themselves.*

Questions for us to ponder together...

1. Why did Jesus want to know what people were saying about His identity?

2. How do you think Jesus felt after hearing what Peter said?

Chapter 40

Jesus Speaks of Easter Week and Peter Tries to Argue

Mark 8:31-33

³¹ *He began to teach them that the Son of Man must suffer many things, and be rejected by the elders, the chief priests, and the scribes, and be killed, and after three days rise again.* ³² *He spoke to them openly. Peter took him, and began to rebuke him.* ³³ *But he, turning around, and seeing his disciples, rebuked Peter, and said, "Get behind me, Satan! For you have in mind not the things of God, but the things of men."*

Let's remember together what we read...

- Most likely, when did this teaching and interaction happen? *During the same journey, either going to or coming back from the region of Caesarea Philippi.*

- During the journey northward to there, what had Peter confessed? *That he believed Jesus was the Christ, the Messiah.*

- Now what did Jesus begin to teach His disciples and followers? *That He would suffer, be rejected by the religious leaders, be killed, and then come back from the dead.*

- Who then took Him aside to have a private conversation? *Peter.*

- What did Peter want to say to Jesus? *That everything He'd just taught couldn't be true; that it wasn't possible for the Christ to go through such things.*

- What—and quite shockingly!—did Jesus then say to Peter? *"Get behind me, satan! For you have in mind not the things of God, but the things of men."*

Questions for us to ponder together...

1. What does it tell you about Jesus that He'd *always known* about the Cross—and yet continued carrying out His ministry?

2. Why do you think He corrected Peter so harshly?

Chapter 41

What It Means to Follow Jesus

Mark 8:34-38

³⁴ *He called the multitude to himself with his disciples, and said to them, "Whoever wants to come after me, let him deny himself, and take up his cross, and follow me. ³⁵ For whoever wants to save his life will lose it; and whoever will lose his life for my sake and the sake of the Good News will save it. ³⁶ For what does it profit a man, to gain the whole world, and forfeit his life? ³⁷ For what will a man give in exchange for his life? ³⁸ For whoever will be ashamed of me and of my words in this adulterous and sinful generation, the Son of Man also will be ashamed of him, when he comes in his Father's glory, with the holy angels."*

Let's remember together what we read...

- Most likely, when did this teaching happen? *Still on the journey, either going to or coming back from Caesarea Philippi; after Peter's confession—and then his rebuke.*

- What did Jesus say anyone who wants to follow Him must do? *Deny himself, take up his cross, and follow Him.*

- What did He say would happen if we try to save our own lives? *We would lose them.*

- What did He say would happen if we lose our lives for His and the Gospel's sake? *We will save them.*

- Do we gain anything by going after gaining the whole world and yet losing our lives/hearts? *No!*

- What does Jesus say about being ashamed of Him and His words? *That if we're ashamed of Him, He'll be ashamed of us.*

Questions for us to ponder together...

1. What does it mean to "deny yourself"?

2. What does it mean for us to "take up our cross"?

3. What does it mean for you to "follow" Jesus?

Chapter 42

Peter, James, and John See What Jesus Is Really Like

Mark 9:1-8

⁹ He said to them, "Most certainly I tell you, there are some standing here who will in no way taste death until they see God's Kingdom come with power."

² After six days Jesus took with him Peter, James, and John, and brought them up onto a high mountain privately by themselves, and he was changed into another form in front of them. ³ His clothing became glistening, exceedingly white, like snow, such as no launderer on earth can whiten them. ⁴ Elijah and Moses appeared to them, and they were talking with Jesus.

⁵ Peter answered Jesus, "Rabbi, it is good for us to be here. Let's make three tents: one for you, one for Moses, and one for Elijah." ⁶ For he didn't know what to say, for they were very afraid.

⁷ A cloud came, overshadowing them, and a voice came out of the cloud, "This is my beloved Son. Listen to him."

⁸ Suddenly looking around, they saw no one with them any more, except Jesus only.

Let's remember together what we read...

- What did Jesus say in the opening of this section? *"I tell you, there are some standing here who will not taste death before they see God's Kingdom coming with power."*

- How many days then went by? *Six days.*

- Who did Jesus take with Him on His hike up the mountain? *Peter, James, and John.*

- What happened to Jesus on that mountaintop? *He was totally changed; His clothing became extremely bright white; He glowed.*

- Who else then appeared alongside Him? *Elijah and Moses. (Parent note: Moses and Elijah represent the fullness of the Law and the Prophets. In other words, it was like the whole Old Testament and the whole Old Covenant were coming to have a meeting with Jesus.)*

- What did Peter, in his excitement, say to Jesus? *In essence, "Teacher, I'm so glad we're here! Let me make three special places for this meeting: one for You, one for Moses, one for Elijah."*

- Why did Peter blurt out this strange idea? *Because all three of the disciples were very afraid.*

- Then what happened? *A cloud passed over, covering over everything, and then a voice spoke out of the cloud.*

- What did the Voice say? *"This is my beloved Son. Listen to him."*

- Does this word from the Father remind you of something from the beginning of our study through Mark?

This is very similar to what the Voice of the Father spoke to Jesus after His baptism by John the Baptist.

- When Peter, James, and John opened their eyes after hearing the Voice, who/what did they see? *Only Jesus—and everything else was back to normal.*

Questions for us to ponder together...

1. Why were Peter, James, and John given this vision of the wonder and splendor of who Jesus really is?

2. What might it mean that Moses and Elijah were there too?

Chapter 43

Jesus Answers Peter, James, and John's Big Question

Mark 9:9-13

⁹ *As they were coming down from the mountain, he commanded them that they should tell no one what things they had seen, until after the Son of Man had risen from the dead.* ¹⁰ *They kept this saying to themselves, questioning what the "rising from the dead" meant.*

¹¹ *They asked him, saying, "Why do the scribes say that Elijah must come first?"*

¹² *He said to them, "Elijah indeed comes first, and restores all things. How is it written about the Son of Man, that he should suffer many things and be despised?* ¹³ *But I tell you that Elijah has come, and they have also done to him whatever they wanted to, even as it is written about him."*

Let's remember together what we read...

- What mountain were they coming down from? *The mountain where Jesus' appearance was totally changed; where Moses and Elijah appeared; where the Voice of the Father spoke of Jesus being His beloved Son.*

- What did Jesus command His friends? *Not to tell anyone what they'd seen up there.*

- When did He say they *could* tell others? *After His Resurrection.*

- Did this make sense to them? *No. They didn't know what He meant by "rising from the dead."*

- What did the disciples then ask Jesus? *"Why do the scribes say that Elijah must come first?"*

- What did Jesus then say about Elijah? *That he had come first; that he was part of God's restoration of the world; and that the world had done to him whatever it wanted to.*

- What does Jesus then say about the Son of Man (meaning, about Himself)? *That He was prophesied to suffer many things and be hated.*

Questions for us to ponder together...

1. Why was Jesus constantly telling people to keep what they'd seen to themselves?

2. What might He have meant when He said that "Elijah *has* come"?

Chapter 44

Jesus Sets a Boy Free and Challenges His Father

Mark 9:14-29

¹⁴ *Coming to the disciples, he saw a great multitude around them, and scribes questioning them.* ¹⁵ *Immediately all the multitude, when they saw him, were greatly amazed, and running to him, greeted him.* ¹⁶ *He asked the scribes, "What are you asking them?"*

¹⁷ *One of the multitude answered, "Teacher, I brought to you my son, who has a mute spirit;* ¹⁸ *and wherever it seizes him, it throws him down, and he foams at the mouth, and grinds his teeth, and wastes away. I asked your disciples to cast it out, and they weren't able."*

¹⁹ *He answered him, "Unbelieving generation, how long shall I be with you? How long shall I bear with you? Bring him to me."*

²⁰ *They brought him to him, and when he saw him, immediately the spirit convulsed him, and he fell on the ground, wallowing and foaming at the mouth.*

²¹ *He asked his father, "How long has it been since this has come to him?"*

He said, "From childhood. ²² *Often it has cast him both into the fire and into the water to destroy him. But if you can do anything, have compassion on us, and help us."*

²³ *Jesus said to him, "If you can believe, all things are possible to him who believes."*

²⁴ Immediately the father of the child cried out with tears, "I believe. Help my unbelief!"

²⁵ When Jesus saw that a multitude came running together, he rebuked the unclean spirit, saying to him, "You mute and deaf spirit, I command you, come out of him, and never enter him again!"

²⁶ After crying out and convulsing him greatly, it came out of him. The boy became like one dead, so much that most of them said, "He is dead." ²⁷ But Jesus took him by the hand, and raised him up; and he arose.

²⁸ When he had come into the house, his disciples asked him privately, "Why couldn't we cast it out?" ²⁹ He said to them, "This kind can come out by nothing, except by prayer and fasting."

Let's remember together what we read...

- Where was Jesus coming from when He came upon this scene? *He was descending from the Mount of Transfiguration—where His appearance had changed, and where Moses and Elijah had appeared.*

- What was happening with the disciples He'd left behind? *They were surrounded by a huge crowd, and some of the scribes were arguing with them.*

- What had all the discussion been about? *About the father who'd brought his son for a healing—whom the disciples had been unable to heal.*

- What was wrong with the boy? *He couldn't speak and would have terrible seizures.*

- Somewhat unexpectedly, what did Jesus then say? *"Unbelieving generation, how long shall I be with you? How long shall I bear with you?"*

- What happened when the boy was brought forward to Jesus? *He had one of his terrible seizures.*

- What did Jesus say to the father when he used the word *"if"* about His power to heal? *"If **you** can believe, all things are possible to him who believes."*

- How did the father respond to this challenge from Jesus? *He cried out with tears in his eyes, "I believe. Help my unbelief!"*

- What did Jesus then do? *Cast out the spirit that was causing the seizures.*

- How did the boy look afterward? *At first, he looked like he was dead.*

- What did Jesus do? *Took him by the hand and raised him up to life and health.*

- Where did Jesus go next? *Into someone's house with His disciples.*

- What did they ask Jesus? *Why they themselves couldn't cast out the unclean spirit.*

- How did Jesus respond? *That that particular unclean spirit could only be cast out through prayer and fasting.*

Questions for us to ponder together...

1. Is there something in your life that Jesus is asking you to believe Him for?

2. Do you believe that *He* can give you the faith to continue believing, to overcome your unbelief?

Chapter 45

Jesus Again Speaks of Easter Week

Mark 9:30-32

³⁰ *They went out from there, and passed through Galilee. He didn't want anyone to know it.* ³¹ *For he was teaching his disciples, and said to them, "The Son of Man is being handed over to the hands of men, and they will kill him; and when he is killed, on the third day he will rise again."* ³² *But they didn't understand the saying, and were afraid to ask him.*

Let's remember together what we read...

- Where were Jesus and His friends going "out" from? *From the Mount of Transfiguration and, afterward, His healing of the boy with seizures.*

- Where did they pass through? *The area surrounding the Sea of Galilee.*

- Did Jesus want everyone to know where He was heading? *No, He "didn't want anyone to know."*

- What was He doing as He traveled? *Teaching His disciples.*

- What, for the second time, was Jesus talking to His friends about? *That He would be handed over to the authorities, killed, and on the third day be raised to life.*

- Did His disciples understand what He was talking about? *No, it didn't make any sense to them.*

Questions for us to ponder together...

1. Do you think *you* would have understood what Jesus was talking about when He talked about Easter week?

2. Why do you think He continually told His friends what was to come?

Chapter 46

Jesus Explains "Greatness" in the Kingdom

Mark 9:33-37

³³ *He came to Capernaum, and when he was in the house he asked them, "What were you arguing among yourselves on the way?"*

³⁴ *But they were silent, for they had disputed with one another on the way about who was the greatest.*

³⁵ *He sat down, and called the twelve; and he said to them, "If any man wants to be first, he shall be last of all, and servant of all."* ³⁶ *He took a little child, and set him in the middle of them. Taking him in his arms, he said to them,* ³⁷ *"Whoever receives one such little child in my name, receives me, and whoever receives me, doesn't receive me, but him who sent me."*

Let's remember together what we read...

- Where did Jesus come back to? *Capernaum.*

- In Capernaum, where did He go? *Into someone's house.*

- What question did Jesus immediately ask His friends? *"What were you arguing about during our journey?"*

- Did the disciples want to answer His question? *No! They were embarrassed because of the topic they'd been discussing.*

- What had they been discussing? *Which of them was the greatest of all.*

- After taking a seat, what did Jesus tell His friends was the exact qualification for becoming "first" or "greatest"? *To make oneself **last** out of everyone, and the servant of **all**.*

- Who did Jesus then call over? *A little child—whom He had stand right there in the middle—and to whom He gave a great big hug!*

- What did He then say about "receiving" little children in His name? *That whoever did so was actually receiving Him.*

- And what did He say about "receiving" Himself (meaning, Jesus)? *That whoever received Him was also receiving His Father who is in Heaven.*

Questions for us to ponder together...

1. What are the reasons that we (and everybody!) so often want to be seen as "greatest"?

2. How does it make you feel when you imagine Jesus calling that little child front and center and then giving him a great big hug?

Chapter 47

Jesus Explains the Kingdom's "For" and "Against"

Mark 9:38-41

38 *John said to him, "Teacher, we saw someone who doesn't follow us casting out demons in your name; and we forbade him, because he doesn't follow us."*

39 *But Jesus said, "Don't forbid him, for there is no one who will do a mighty work in my name, and be able quickly to speak evil of me.* 40 *For whoever is not against us is on our side.* 41 *For whoever will give you a cup of water to drink in my name, because you are Christ's, most certainly I tell you, he will in no way lose his reward."*

Let's remember together what we read...

- Who spoke up with a comment for Jesus? *John—the brother of James, the son of Zebedee—the author of the Gospel "John."*

- What did John tell Jesus about? *That he'd seen someone who wasn't part of their inner circle casting out demons in Jesus' name, and that he (John) had told the person to stop because they weren't part of the Twelve.*

- What did Jesus say about John's response to that person? *That he didn't need to stop such a person, because clearly that power was coming from Jesus; that you can't do that kind of work and then turn around and speak evil of Jesus.*

- What did Jesus say about "whoever is not against us"? *That they are on our side.*

- What did Jesus say about someone who will give you a cup of water to drink in His name? *That if they do so because you belong to Him, they will "in no way lose [their] reward."*

Questions for us to ponder together...

1. What are the reasons that we (and everybody!) so often want to create divisions: "us" vs. "them"?

2. What does Jesus' response to John tell us about Jesus' desire for spiritual unity in the Kingdom of Heaven?

Chapter 48

Jesus Explains How Careful His Followers Must Be

Mark 9:42-50

[42] *"Whoever will cause one of these little ones who believe in me to stumble, it would be better for him if he were thrown into the sea with a millstone hung around his neck.* [43] *If your hand causes you to stumble, cut it off. It is better for you to enter into life maimed, rather than having your two hands to go into Gehenna,[1] into the unquenchable fire,* [44] *'where their worm doesn't die, and the fire is not quenched.'* [45] *If your foot causes you to stumble, cut it off. It is better for you to enter into life lame, rather than having your two feet to be cast into Gehenna, into the fire that will never be quenched—*[46] *'where their worm doesn't die, and the fire is not quenched.'* [47] *If your eye causes you to stumble, cast it out. It is better for you to enter into God's Kingdom with one eye, rather than having two eyes to be cast into the Gehenna of fire,* [48] *'where their worm doesn't die, and the fire is not quenched.'* [49] *For everyone will be salted with fire, and every sacrifice will be seasoned with salt.* [50] *Salt is good, but if the salt has lost its saltiness, with what will you season it? Have salt in yourselves, and be at peace with one another."*

---

1   Another name, in Hebrew culture, for hell.

Let's remember together what we read...

- What did Jesus tell His friends about causing a "little one" to stumble in their belief? *That it would be better to be thrown in the sea with a huge stone tied around your neck!*

- What did Jesus say about your hand, if it should be the cause of your stumbling? *That you should cut it off! (Parent note: Obviously you'll want to help your child understand that Jesus doesn't **literally** want you to cut off your hand; He is heightening our desire to be holy as we follow Him.)*

- What did Jesus say about your foot, if it should be the cause of your stumbling? *That you should cut it off! (Parent note: Again you'll want to help your child understand that Jesus doesn't **literally** want you to cut off your foot; He is heightening our desire to be holy as we follow Him.)*

- What did Jesus say about your eye, if it should be the cause of your stumbling? *That you should pluck it out and throw it away! (Parent note: Yet again you'll want to help your child understand that Jesus doesn't **literally** want you to pluck out your eye; He is heightening our desire to be holy as we follow Him.)*

- What are some of the things that Jesus says about salt? *That we will be "salted" (or seasoned) with fire; that every sacrifice will be seasoned with salt; that salt is good, but only if it stays salty; that we need to have salt in us.*

- Fill in the blank: Jesus says we need to "be at _____ with one another." *Peace.*

Questions for us to ponder together...

1. What is Jesus' purpose in being so harsh about our hands, feet, and eyes as He's teaching us about holiness?

2. What do you think He means when He talks about "salt" and being "seasoned with salt"?

Chapter 49

Jesus Explains How Seriously God Takes Marriage

Mark 10:1-12

[1] *He arose from there and came into the borders of Judea and beyond the Jordan. Multitudes came together to him again. As he usually did, he was again teaching them.* [2] *Pharisees came to him testing him, and asked him, "Is it lawful for a man to divorce his wife?"*

[3] *He answered, "What did Moses command you?"*

[4] *They said, "Moses allowed a certificate of divorce to be written, and to divorce her."*

[5] *But Jesus said to them, "For your hardness of heart, he wrote you this commandment.* [6] *But from the beginning of the creation, God made them male and female.* [7] *For this cause a man will leave his father and mother, and will join to his wife,* [8] *and the two will become one flesh, so that they are no longer two, but one flesh.* [9] *What therefore God has joined together, let no man separate."*

[10] *In the house, his disciples asked him again about the same matter.* [11] *He said to them, "Whoever divorces his wife, and marries another, commits adultery against her.* [12] *If a woman herself divorces her husband, and marries another, she commits adultery."*

Let's remember together what we read...

- Where had Jesus been before He traveled south in this narrative? *At Capernaum in Galilee.*

- Where are we told He traveled to, here? *Into Judea, where He went to the other side of the Jordan River.*

- Who came to see Him on His arrival? *Multitudes of people.*

- What did He begin doing for the great crowds? *Teaching them.*

- Who are we told came to test Him? *Some Pharisees.*

- What was the Pharisee's test question? *"Is it lawful for a man to divorce his wife?"*

- What question did Jesus ask in return? *"What did Moses (i.e. the Law) command you?"*

- What did the Pharisees say in response? *That Moses allowed a certificate of divorce to be written, i.e. that divorce was allowed.*

- Why did Jesus say Moses wrote this commandment? *Because of the people's "hardness of heart."*

- What does Jesus say was the Father's original intention for marriage? *That, being made male and female, people would leave behind their own parents and be married, becoming one flesh, and then never separate.*

- Where did they go after Jesus answered the Pharisees? *Into someone's house.*

- When the disciples asked Jesus about His words, what did He say to them? *That divorcing and remarrying is like being unfaithful in God's sight. (Parent note: Because, in our day and age, so many children know children who are part of divorced families, this is an important moment to talk about how we are not called to judge; and also about God's mercy, even to those who are in broken situations.)*

Questions for us to ponder together...

1. How seriously does Jesus mean for us to take the vows of marriage?

2. What does it mean that it is *God* who "joins together" husbands and wives?

Chapter 50

Jesus, Little Children, and the Kingdom

Mark 10:13-16

¹³ *They were bringing to him little children, that he should touch them, but the disciples rebuked those who were bringing them.* ¹⁴ *But when Jesus saw it, he was moved with indignation, and said to them, "Allow the little children to come to me! Don't forbid them, for God's Kingdom belongs to such as these.* ¹⁵ *Most certainly I tell you, whoever will not receive God's Kingdom like a little child, he will in no way enter into it."* ¹⁶ *He took them in his arms, and blessed them, laying his hands on them.*

Let's remember together what we read...

- Who was being brought to Jesus? *Little children.*

- Why were people bringing these little children to Him? *So that He would touch them, i.e. bless them.*

- How did the disciples react to their being brought? *They "rebuked"—tried to turn away—those who were bringing them.*

- How did Jesus feel when He saw what His disciples were doing? *He was very angry—"moved with indignation."*

- What did Jesus say about the little children and God's Kingdom? *That it **belongs** to these little ones!*

- What did He say about people who *won't* receive God's Kingdom like a little child? *That they will never enter into it!*

- Then what did He do for the little children? *He wrapped them up in a big hug, blessed them, and laid His hands on them.*

Questions for us to ponder together...

1. How would you feel about being wrapped up in a hug, blessed, and then having Jesus lay His hands upon you?

2. What do you think it means to "receive God's Kingdom like a little child"?

Chapter 51

Jesus and the "Rich Young Ruler"

Mark 10:17-22

¹⁷ *As he was going out into the way, one ran to him, knelt before him, and asked him, "Good Teacher, what shall I do that I may inherit eternal life?"*

¹⁸ *Jesus said to him, "Why do you call me good? No one is good except one—God. ¹⁹ You know the commandments: 'Do not murder,' 'Do not commit adultery,' 'Do not steal,' 'Do not give false testimony,' 'Do not defraud,' 'Honor your father and mother.'"*

²⁰ *He said to him, "Teacher, I have observed all these things from my youth."*

²¹ *Jesus looking at him loved him, and said to him, "One thing you lack. Go, sell whatever you have, and give to the poor, and you will have treasure in heaven; and come, follow me, taking up the cross."*

²² *But his face fell at that saying, and he went away sorrowful, for he was one who had great possessions.*

Let's remember together what we read...

- What did the man do when he came to ask Jesus his question? *Ran up to Him and knelt down before Him.*

- And what was the man's question? *"Good Teacher, what shall I do that I may inherit eternal life?"*

- What did Jesus say immediately in response? *"Why do you call me good? No one is good except one—God."*

- Then how did Jesus answer the man's question? *"You know the commandments: 'Do not murder,' 'Do not commit adultery,' 'Do not steal,' 'Do not give false testimony,' 'Do not defraud,' 'Honor your father and mother.'"*

- What did the man say to this? *"Teacher, I have observed all these things from my youth."*

- How did Jesus feel about the man when He heard him say this? *He "loved him."*

- What did Jesus then say to the man about what was still needed? *That he should sell everything he had, give it to the poor (by which he would "lay up treasure in heaven"), and then come and follow Jesus, taking up his cross.*

- How did the man look after hearing this? *Sad and sorrowful.*

- Why? *Because he was very wealthy and didn't want to give away what he had.*

Questions for us to ponder together...

1. Why do you think Jesus' heart was so warmed toward this man?

2. What does it mean to you—right now—to "follow" Jesus?

Chapter 52

Jesus Explains How Money and Possessions Can Get in the Way

Mark 10:23-27

23 *Jesus looked around [after the "rich young ruler" left] , and said to his disciples, "How difficult it is for those who have riches to enter into God's Kingdom!"*

24 *The disciples were amazed at his words. But Jesus answered again, "Children, how hard it is for those who trust in riches to enter into God's Kingdom!* 25 *It is easier for a camel to go through a needle's eye than for a rich man to enter into God's Kingdom."*

26 *They were exceedingly astonished, saying to him, "Then who can be saved?"*

27 *Jesus, looking at them, said, "With men it is impossible, but not with God, for all things are possible with God."*

Let's remember together what we read...

- Who had just walked away at the beginning of this section? *The "rich young ruler" who didn't want to give up his possessions to follow Jesus.*

- What did Jesus say to His disciples as He watched that man leave? *"How difficult it is for those who have riches to enter into God's Kingdom!"*

- How did the disciples feel when they heard Jesus' words? *They were amazed.*

- According to Jesus, is it easy or hard for those who trust in riches to enter into the Kingdom of God? *Hard.*

- What would be easier for a camel to go through than for a rich man to enter the Kingdom of God? *The eye of a needle.*

- The disciples, astonished by this, then asked what of Jesus? *"Then who can be saved?"*

- What did Jesus say about the impossible and the possible? *That with men it is impossible, but with God anything is possible.*

Questions for us to ponder together...

1. Why do money, possessions, and riches make it difficult for our hearts to focus on the Kingdom of God?

2. How does it make you feel that "all things are possible with God"?

Chapter 53

Jesus Speaks of the Benefits of Following Him

Mark 10:28-31

28 *Peter began to tell him, "Behold, we have left all, and have followed you."*

29 *Jesus said, "Most certainly I tell you, there is no one who has left house, or brothers, or sisters, or father, or mother, or wife, or children, or land, for my sake, and for the sake of the Good News,* 30 *but he will receive one hundred times more now in this time: houses, brothers, sisters, mothers, children, and land, with persecutions; and in the age to come eternal life.* 31 *But many who are first will be last; and the last first."*

Let's remember together what we read...

- When did this teaching occur? *Right after the "rich young ruler" departed from Jesus, and after Jesus talked about the relationship between riches and the Kingdom of God.*

- Who then spoke up? *Peter.*

- What did Peter remind Jesus of? *That he and the other disciples had left everything to come follow Him.*

- What are all of the things His disciples had left that Jesus then talks about? *Houses, brothers, sisters, fathers, mothers, wives, children, and land.*

- Why had His disciples left those behind? *For His sake and for the sake of the Good News (the Gospel).*

- How much does Jesus say they'll receive in return for leaving all that behind? *One hundred times more.*

- And what else will they receive? *Persecutions—and eternal life.*

- What will happen to "the first"? *They will be last.*

- What will happen to "the last"? *They will be first.*

Questions for us to ponder together...

1. What has our family received because of following Jesus?

2. How would you explain what "eternal life" is?

Chapter 54

Jesus Yet Again Speaks of Easter Week

Mark 10:32-34

³² *They were on the way, going up to Jerusalem; and Jesus was going in front of them, and they were amazed; and those who followed were afraid. He again took the twelve, and began to tell them the things that were going to happen to him.* ³³ *"Behold, we are going up to Jerusalem. The Son of Man will be delivered to the chief priests and the scribes. They will condemn him to death, and will deliver him to the Gentiles.* ³⁴ *They will mock him, spit on him, scourge him, and kill him. On the third day he will rise again."*

Let's remember together what we read...

- Where were Jesus and His disciples on their way to? *Up to Jerusalem, the capital city.*

- Where was Jesus walking, with respect to His disciples? *Boldly, up in front.*

- How did this make the disciples feel? *Amazed.*

- And how did the crowds following behind them feel? *Afraid.*

- Who did Jesus then draw to the side for a private conversation? *The Twelve.*

- What did He tell them—now for the third time? *That, going up to Jerusalem, He would be delivered to the religious authorities; that He would be condemned to death; that He would be mocked and abused before dying; and that, after three days, He would rise again.*

Questions for us to ponder together...

1. As Jesus boldly turned to Jerusalem, how do you think *you* would've been feeling?

2. When He describes His trials to come, what most sticks out to you?

Chapter 55

Jesus and a Request from James and John

Mark 10:35-40

³⁵ *James and John, the sons of Zebedee, came near to him, saying, "Teacher, we want you to do for us whatever we will ask."*

³⁶ *He said to them, "What do you want me to do for you?"*

³⁷ *They said to him, "Grant to us that we may sit, one at your right hand, and one at your left hand, in your glory."*

³⁸ *But Jesus said to them, "You don't know what you are asking. Are you able to drink the cup that I drink, and to be baptized with the baptism that I am baptized with?"*

³⁹ *They said to him, "We are able."*

Jesus said to them, "You shall indeed drink the cup that I drink, and you shall be baptized with the baptism that I am baptized with; ⁴⁰ *but to sit at my right hand and at my left hand is not mine to give, but for whom it has been prepared."*

Let's remember together what we read...

- What two disciples came and approached Jesus on their own? *James and John, the sons of Zebedee.*

- What did they ask of Jesus? *That they could sit one on each side of Him when He came into His glory.*

- Did Jesus think they understood what they were asking of Him? *No.*

- What are the two things Jesus asked if they were able and willing to do? *To drink the cup He would drink, and be baptized with the baptism He must undergo.*

- How did they respond? *"We are able."*

- What did Jesus say about them drinking the cup and being baptized with His baptism? *That indeed they would have to go through those things.*

- But was He able to allow them to have the right-hand and left-hand spots beside His throne? *No, He said. Those were for the ones "for whom it has been prepared."*

Questions for us to ponder together...

1. What do you think drove James and John to make this request of Jesus?

2. What do you think Jesus meant by His "cup" and the "baptism" He was going to go through?

Chapter 56

Jesus Explains Greatness and Service

Mark 10:41-45

⁴¹ *When the ten heard [about James and John wanting places of honor alongside Jesus], they began to be indignant toward James and John.*

⁴² *Jesus summoned them, and said to them, "You know that they who are recognized as rulers over the nations lord it over them, and their great ones exercise authority over them.* ⁴³ *But it shall not be so among you, but whoever wants to become great among you shall be your servant.* ⁴⁴ *Whoever of you wants to become first among you, shall be bondservant of all.* ⁴⁵ *For the Son of Man also came not to be served, but to serve, and to give his life as a ransom for many."*

Let's remember together what we read...

- When did this scene and teaching occur? *Right after James and John asked to have the right- and left-hand places beside Jesus' throne.*

- How did the other ten disciples feel about the brothers' request? *They were furious at James and John.*

- What did Jesus say about the way worldly rulers and "great" people act other toward others? *That they "lord it over" other people and "exercise authority over" their fellow man.*

- Is that how it's meant to be in the Kingdom of Heaven? *No!*

- In the Kingdom of Heaven, how do you become "great"? *By being a servant.*

- In the Kingdom of Heaven, how do you become "first"? *By being the "bondservant of all."*

- Did Jesus come to *be* served? *No, He came **to** serve.*

- What was He going to give His life for? *To be a ransom for many, i.e. for everyone.*

Questions for us to ponder together...

1. What are some practical ways we can learn to honor Jesus by making ourselves less, by being a servant of others?

2. Is there someone we are currently angry with that we can choose to forgive?

Chapter 57

Jesus Heals a Blind Man in Jericho

Mark 10:46-52

⁴⁶ *They came to Jericho. As he went out from Jericho, with his disciples and a great multitude, the son of Timaeus, Bartimaeus, a blind beggar, was sitting by the road.* ⁴⁷ *When he heard that it was Jesus the Nazarene, he began to cry out, and say, "Jesus, you son of David, have mercy on me!"* ⁴⁸ *Many rebuked him, that he should be quiet, but he cried out much more, "You son of David, have mercy on me!"*

⁴⁹ *Jesus stood still, and said, "Call him."*

They called the blind man, saying to him, "Cheer up! Get up. He is calling you!"

⁵⁰ *He, casting away his cloak, sprang up, and came to Jesus.*

⁵¹ *Jesus asked him, "What do you want me to do for you?"*

The blind man said to him, "Rabboni, that I may see again."

⁵² *Jesus said to him, "Go your way. Your faith has made you well." Immediately he received his sight, and followed Jesus on the way.*

Let's remember together what we read...

- What town was Jesus passing through? *Jericho.*

- Who was surrounding Him? *His disciples and a great multitude.*

- Who happened to be sitting there along the road? *Bartimaeus, a blind beggar.*

- What did Bartimaeus do when he heard that it was Jesus coming along? *He began shouting loudly, "Jesus, you son of David, have mercy on me!"*

- Did the people around Bartimaeus appreciate his loud shouting? *No, they told him to keep quiet!*

- Did Bartimaeus listen to them? *No! He only shouted the same thing more!*

- In the midst of the crowd, what did Jesus do? *Stopped where He was and asked the people to get Bartimaeus to come.*

- What did Jesus ask Bartimaeus when he approached? *"What do you want me to do for you?"*

- What did Bartimaeus want Jesus to do for him? *To give him the gift of sight.*

- What did Jesus say in response? *"Go your way. Your faith has made you well."*

- What happened to Bartimaeus? *Suddenly, he could see!*

- And where did Bartimaeus go? *He followed Jesus where He was going.*

Questions for us to ponder together...

1. What do you like best about this moment?

2. How does it make you feel when you see Jesus stopping in the midst of the enormous crowd to have this one interaction with Bartimaeus?

Chapter 58

Jesus Enters
Jerusalem Gloriously

Mark 11:1-10

¹¹ *When they came near to Jerusalem, to Bethphage and Bethany, at the Mount of Olives, he sent two of his disciples,* ² *and said to them, "Go your way into the village that is opposite you. Immediately as you enter into it, you will find a young donkey tied, on which no one has sat. Untie him, and bring him.* ³ *If anyone asks you, 'Why are you doing this?' say, 'The Lord needs him;' and immediately he will send him back here."*

⁴ *They went away, and found a young donkey tied at the door outside in the open street, and they untied him.* ⁵ *Some of those who stood there asked them, "What are you doing, untying the young donkey?"* ⁶ *They said to them just as Jesus had said, and they let them go.*

⁷ *They brought the young donkey to Jesus, and threw their garments on it, and Jesus sat on it.* ⁸ *Many spread their garments on the way, and others were cutting down branches from the trees, and spreading them on the road.* ⁹ *Those who went in front, and those who followed, cried out, "Hosanna! Blessed is he who comes in the name of the Lord!* ¹⁰ *Blessed is the kingdom of our father David that is coming in the name of the Lord! Hosanna in the highest!"*

Let's remember together what we read...

- Where were they *"near to"* when this narrative began? *Jerusalem, the capital city.*

- What were the names of the two villages to which Jesus was arriving? *Bethphage and Bethany.*

- What was the name of the mountain right there? *The Mount of Olives.*

- How many disciples did He send off on an important errand? *Two.*

- What were they supposed to go find and what were they supposed to do? *A young donkey tied up, which they were supposed to bring back to Him.*

- What should they say if someone tried to stop them or asked them what they were doing with the donkey? *"The Lord needs him."*

- Did everything happen exactly as Jesus described when they went on this errand? *Exactly!*

- When they brought the donkey to Jesus, what did they do? *Threw their outer garments on it and got Jesus up on its back.*

- As they then entered into Jerusalem, with Jesus riding atop the donkey, what did the crowds do? *Spread their garments on the roadway; cut down palm branches from trees and spread them on the road too. (Parent note: It is in John's Gospel that "palm branches" are specified, from which we get the name "Palm Sunday.")*

- What did the crowds shout as Jesus rode into the city? *"Hosanna! Blessed is He who comes in the name of the Lord! Blessed is the kingdom of our father David that is coming in the name of the Lord! Hosanna in the highest!"* (Parent note: "Hosanna!" means "Please save us!")

Questions for us to ponder together...

1. What do you think the crowds and the disciples thought Jesus' entry into Jerusalem might mean?

2. What kind of "saving" work was Jesus actually preparing to do for them?

Chapter 59

Jesus, the Fig Tree, and the Temple

Mark 11:11-19

11 *Jesus entered into the temple in Jerusalem. When he had looked around at everything, it being now evening, he went out to Bethany with the twelve.*

12 *The next day, when they had come out from Bethany, he was hungry.* 13 *Seeing a fig tree afar off having leaves, he came to see if perhaps he might find anything on it. When he came to it, he found nothing but leaves, for it was not the season for figs.* 14 *Jesus told it, "May no one ever eat fruit from you again!" and his disciples heard it.*

15 *They came to Jerusalem, and Jesus entered into the temple, and began to throw out those who sold and those who bought in the temple, and overthrew the money changers' tables, and the seats of those who sold the doves.* 16 *He would not allow anyone to carry a container through the temple.* 17 *He taught, saying to them, "Isn't it written, 'My house will be called a house of prayer for all the nations?' But you have made it a den of robbers!"*

18 *The chief priests and the scribes heard it, and sought how they might destroy him. For they feared him, because all the multitude was astonished at his teaching.*

19 *When evening came, he went out of the city.*

Let's remember together what we read...

- What happened right before this section? *Jesus' triumphal entry into Jerusalem on the back of a donkey, as the crowds shouted and praised Him.*

- Where did He then go? *Into the temple at the heart of Jerusalem.*

- What did He do on this first evening? *Nothing, other than "looking around."*

- Where did He spend that night with the Twelve? *In the village of Bethany.*

- The next morning, what did Jesus happen to see? *A fig tree.*

- Why did He approach it? *Because, we're told, "he was hungry."*

- Did the fig tree have any fruit for Him to eat? *No.*

- What did Jesus say to the tree? *"May no one ever eat fruit from you again!"*

- Then, entering Jerusalem, where did Jesus go? *Into the temple.*

- And what did He do there? *He threw out the sellers and buyers in the courtyard and flipped over the money changers' tables and the seats of those who sold sacrificial doves, and He wouldn't let anyone pass through carrying a container.*

- And what did He say after He'd done all this? *"My house will be called a house of prayer for all the nations. But you have made it a den of robbers!"*

- Who was watching His actions and marking His words? *The chief priests and scribes.*

- What did they start plotting to do? *To kill Him.*
- Why? *Because they were afraid of Him and because the people were amazed at His teachings.*
- Did Jesus stay in the city that night? *No, He went back out.*

Questions for us to ponder together...

1. Why was Jesus upset with the fig tree?
2. Why was Jesus upset with the sellers in the temple?

Chapter 60

Jesus, the Fig Tree, and Faith

Mark 11:20-26

20 *As they passed by in the morning, they saw the fig tree withered away from the roots.* 21 *Peter, remembering, said to him, "Rabbi, look! The fig tree which you cursed has withered away."*

22 *Jesus answered them, "Have faith in God.* 23 *For most certainly I tell you, whoever may tell this mountain, 'Be taken up and cast into the sea,' and doesn't doubt in his heart, but believes that what he says is happening; he shall have whatever he says.* 24 *Therefore I tell you, all things whatever you pray and ask for, believe that you have received them, and you shall have them.* 25 *Whenever you stand praying, forgive, if you have anything against anyone; so that your Father, who is in heaven, may also forgive you your transgressions.* 26 *But if you do not forgive, neither will your Father in heaven forgive your transgressions."*

Let's remember together what we read...

- When did this take place? *The day after He cursed the fig tree and ended the temple commerce; two days after the Triumphal Entry into Jerusalem.*

- On this morning, what did His disciples notice? *That the fig tree had withered all the way down to its roots.*

- Who brought this to Jesus' attention? *Peter.*

- What immediate command did Jesus give to Peter and the others? *"Have faith in God."*

- What does Jesus say will happen to a mountain if you have faith? *It can be taken up and cast into the sea!*

- What does Jesus say we should we do when we are praying about anything? *Believe that it is already done!*

- Additionally, what does Jesus say we need to do when we are preparing to pray? *Forgive anyone we are holding anything against.*

- Why does He say our forgiveness of others is so important? *It's part of how we receive our own forgiveness from the Father.*

- What does He say will happen if we *won't* forgive others? *We will not be forgiven!*

Questions for us to ponder together...

1. What is something *big* you've been praying about lately?

2. Is there someone in your life you still need to forgive?

Chapter 61

Jesus Challenges a Question with a Question

Mark 11:27-33

27 *They came again to Jerusalem, and as he was walking in the temple, the chief priests, the scribes, and the elders came to him,* 28 *and they began saying to him, "By what authority do you do these things? Or who gave you this authority to do these things?"*

29 *Jesus said to them, "I will ask you one question. Answer me, and I will tell you by what authority I do these things.* 30 *The baptism of John—was it from heaven, or from men? Answer me."*

31 *They reasoned with themselves, saying, "If we should say, 'From heaven;' he will say, 'Why then did you not believe him?'* 32 *If we should say, 'From men'"—they feared the people, for all held John to really be a prophet.* 33 *They answered Jesus, "We don't know."*

Jesus said to them, "Neither do I tell you by what authority I do these things."

Let's remember together what we read...

- Where was Jesus entering into? *The temple in Jerusalem.*

- Who came up to Him? *The chief priests, scribes, and some of the elders of the people.*

- What question(s) did they ask Him? *"By what authority do you do these things? Who gave you this authority to do these things?"*

- How did Jesus respond to their questions? *With a question!*

- What was Jesus' question? *"John's baptism—was it from Heaven or from men?"*

- What were the religious leaders' fears about their two possible responses? *If they said, "From Heaven," Jesus would ask why they hadn't believed; if they said, "From men," the people would be angry at them.*

- So what instead did they say? *"We don't know."*

- And how did Jesus respond to their answer? *By saying, in essence, "In that case, I won't answer your question!"*

Questions for us to ponder together...

1. Why is it so powerful when, instead of arguing, we return a question with a question?

2. By whose "authority" *was* Jesus doing what He was doing?

Chapter 62

Jesus and the Parable of the Vineyard

Mark 12:1-12

¹ *He began to speak to them in parables. "A man planted a vineyard, put a hedge around it, dug a pit for the wine press, built a tower, rented it out to a farmer, and went into another country.* ² *When it was time, he sent a servant to the farmer to get from the farmer his share of the fruit of the vineyard.* ³ *They took him, beat him, and sent him away empty.* ⁴ *Again, he sent another servant to them; and they threw stones at him, wounded him in the head, and sent him away shamefully treated.* ⁵ *Again he sent another; and they killed him; and many others, beating some, and killing some.* ⁶ *Therefore still having one, his beloved son, he sent him last to them, saying, 'They will respect my son.'* ⁷ *But those farmers said among themselves, 'This is the heir. Come, let's kill him, and the inheritance will be ours.'* ⁸ *They took him, killed him, and cast him out of the vineyard.* ⁹ *What therefore will the lord of the vineyard do? He will come and destroy the farmers, and will give the vineyard to others.* ¹⁰ *Haven't you even read this Scripture:*

'The stone which the builders rejected was made the head of the corner.
¹¹ *This was from the Lord. It is marvelous in our eyes'?"*

[12] *They tried to seize him, but they feared the multitude; for they perceived that he spoke the parable against them. They left him, and went away.*

Let's remember together what we read...

- When did this teaching happen? *On the same day when the religious leaders challenged Jesus with the question of His authority.*

- What is the name of the special stories Jesus so often used in His teachings? *Parables.*

- In this parable, what did the man create for himself? *A vineyard.*

- When he left for another country, who did he leave in charge of the vineyard? *A farmer who rented the property.*

- At a certain time, what did the owner send his servant to receive? *His share of the vineyard's fruit.*

- What did the renter and his people do to that servant? *Beat him up and sent him back with nothing.*

- Did the owner give up? *No. He sent many more servants—who were likewise beat up, hurt, even killed.*

- Who did the owner decide to send last? *His own son.*

- But what did the renter and his people do to the owner's son? *They killed him thinking that with him dead they might take over the vineyard for themselves.*

- What did Jesus say would happen to that wicked renter? *He would be destroyed and the owner would find a good tenant for his vineyard.*

- Who was this parable seemingly spoken against? *The religious leaders who had just been challenging Jesus.*

- How did they feel about Jesus in this moment? *Furious! They wanted to seize Him, but didn't—only because they feared the crowds.*

Questions for us to ponder together...

1. When you think about all that happened in Jesus' parable, what do you think it's about?

2. What is the "fruit" that Jesus wants to see in our lives?

Chapter 63

Jesus and Taxes

Mark 12:13-17

[13] *They sent some of the Pharisees and the Herodians to him, that they might trap him with words.* [14] *When they had come, they asked him, "Teacher, we know that you are honest, and don't defer to anyone; for you aren't partial to anyone, but truly teach the way of God. Is it lawful to pay taxes to Caesar, or not?* [15] *Shall we give, or shall we not give?"*

But he, knowing their hypocrisy, said to them, "Why do you test me? Bring me a denarius, that I may see it."

[16] *They brought it.*

He said to them, "Whose is this image and inscription?"

They said to him, "Caesar's."

[17] *Jesus answered them, "Render to Caesar the things that are Caesar's, and to God the things that are God's."*

They marveled greatly at him.

Let's remember together what we read...

- Now who came to test Jesus with a difficult question? *Some of the Pharisees and others who were devoted to Herod.*

- What were the flattering words these men spoke to Jesus, possibly hoping to put Him off His guard? *That He was honest and didn't defer to anyone; that He was impartial and truly taught God's way.*

- And then, what was their "trap" question? *"It is lawful to pay taxes to Caesar, or not?"*

- What, we are told, did Jesus know about these men? *Their "hypocrisy," meaning, that they had two different sides—two different faces (just like a coin!).*

- What did Jesus ask them to give Him? *A denarius coin.*

- What did He ask them about the coin? *Whose image and inscription were on it.*

- What did they answer Jesus? *"Caesar's."*

- So what was Jesus' final word to them on the subject? *"Then give to Caesar what belongs to Caesar, and to God what belongs to God."*

- How did this leave the Pharisees and Herodians feelings? *Marveling at His answer.*

Questions for us to ponder together...

1. While our world seems so consumed with money, wealth, and possessions, how did Jesus seem to view them?

2. What do you think "belongs to God"—or, in other words, what do we "owe" God?

Chapter 64

Jesus and Life After Death

Mark 12:18-27

[18] *Some Sadducees, who say that there is no resurrection, came to him. They asked him, saying,* [19] *"Teacher, Moses wrote to us, 'If a man's brother dies, and leaves a wife behind him, and leaves no children, that his brother should take his wife, and raise up offspring for his brother.'* [20] *There were seven brothers. The first took a wife, and dying left no offspring.* [21] *The second took her, and died, leaving no children behind him. The third likewise;* [22] *and the seven took her and left no children. Last of all the woman also died.* [23] *In the resurrection, when they rise, whose wife will she be of them? For the seven had her as a wife."*

[24] *Jesus answered them, "Isn't this because you are mistaken, not knowing the Scriptures, nor the power of God?* [25] *For when they will rise from the dead, they neither marry, nor are given in marriage, but are like angels in heaven.* [26] *But about the dead, that they are raised; haven't you read in the book of Moses, about the Bush, how God spoke to him, saying, 'I am the God of Abraham, the God of Isaac, and the God of Jacob'?* [27] *He is not the God of the dead, but of the living. You are therefore badly mistaken."*

Let's remember together what we read...

- Who came next to test Jesus? *The Sadducees.*
- What are we told they *didn't* believe in? *The resurrection of the dead.*
- What commandment of Moses did they want to test Jesus about? *That if a man dies his brother should marry his widow and raise their children on behalf of his brother.*
- In the Sadducees' question, how many brothers were there? *Seven.*
- How many women ended up being married to all seven? *Just one!*
- What was the Sadducees' final question about their made-up story? *After the woman dies and she and all those brothers are resurrected, whose wife will she be considered to be?*
- What question did Jesus immediately ask them in return? *"Aren't you just mistaken, and don't know the Scriptures, or even the power of God?"*
- What does Jesus say about how people will be in Heaven? *They won't be married, like on earth, but will be like the angels.*
- When He quotes from Exodus, what is Jesus trying to say about how God views people? *That they are all as if alive to Him, all the time.*

Questions for us to ponder together...

1. What do we learn about Jesus' personality when we see people testing Him with such silly, ridiculous questions?

2. How does it make you feel to know that the Living God is truly watching over you?

Chapter 65

Jesus and the Greatest Commandment

Mark 12:28-34

28 *One of the scribes came, and heard them questioning together, and knowing that he had answered them well, asked him, "Which commandment is the greatest of all?"*

29 *Jesus answered, "The greatest is, 'Hear, Israel, the Lord our God, the Lord is one:* 30 *you shall love the Lord your God with all your heart, and with all your soul, and with all your mind, and with all your strength.' This is the first commandment.* 31 *The second is like this, 'You shall love your neighbor as yourself.' There is no other commandment greater than these."*

32 *The scribe said to him, "Truly, teacher, you have said well that he is one, and there is none other but he,* 33 *and to love him with all the heart, and with all the understanding, with all the soul, and with all the strength, and to love his neighbor as himself, is more important than all whole burnt offerings and sacrifices."*

34 *When Jesus saw that he answered wisely, he said to him, "You are not far from God's Kingdom."*

No one dared ask him any question after that.

Let's remember together what we read...

- Who came to Jesus next? *One of the scribes.*

- What did this man overhear? *The way Jesus was tested by the Pharisees, Herodians, and Sadducees, and how He answered them so well.*

- What was this scribe's question for Jesus? *"Which commandment is the greatest of all?"*

- What was Jesus' two-part answer? *Love the Lord your God with all your heart, all your soul, all your mind, all your strength; and love your neighbor as you love yourself.*

- How did the scribe respond to Jesus' answer? *By complimenting how He'd answered, and by agreeing that loving God and loving others is more important than all the religious offerings anyone ever offered.*

- And how did Jesus respond to the scribe's answer? *By saying he was not far from the Kingdom of God.*

- How did everyone feel about questioning Jesus any further now? *They didn't dare.*

Questions for us to ponder together...

1. Why do you think Jesus' response to "the greatest commandment" question was to answer with *two* responses?

2. Is loving others one of the clearest ways we can learn to love God?

Chapter 66

Jesus, the "Son of David"

Mark 12:35-37

^{35} *Jesus responded, as he taught in the temple, "How is it that the scribes say that the Christ is the son of David?* ^{36} *For David himself said in the Holy Spirit,*

'The Lord said to my Lord,
"Sit at my right hand,
until I make your enemies the footstool of your feet."'

^{37} *Therefore David himself calls him Lord, so how can he be his son?"*

The common people heard him gladly.

Let's remember together what we read...

- When does Jesus have this interaction? *It would seem to be on the same day He was questioned by the Pharisees, Herodians, Sadducees, and one lone scribe.*

- What is the name people called Jesus that Jesus Himself asks them about? *The "son of David."*

- Who does Jesus say that David himself spoke by? *The Holy Spirit.*

- What does Jesus say David called Him (meaning, Jesus)? *"Lord."*

- So what is Jesus' conclusion in this short exchange? *That if He is David's "Lord," He can't really, truly be His "son."*

- How did the people hearing Jesus feel about hearing Him teach? *They were glad.*

Questions for us to ponder together...

1. Why do you think Jesus made this particular point for the people?

2. What is one of Jesus' teachings that makes *you* "glad"?

Chapter 67

Jesus versus the Attitude of the Religious Leaders

Mark 12:38-40

38 *In his teaching he said to them, "Beware of the scribes, who like to walk in long robes, and to get greetings in the marketplaces,* 39 *and the best seats in the synagogues, and the best places at feasts:* 40 *those who devour widows' houses, and for a pretense make long prayers. These will receive greater condemnation."*

Let's remember together what we read...

- Who did Jesus tell the crowds to be careful of? *The scribes.*

- What were some of the things that Jesus said the scribes liked to do? *To wear long (and probably fancy!) robes; to be greeted importantly in the market; to have the best seats in the synagogue and at feasts; to make use of widows' money; to offer up long prayers to God.*

- What does Jesus say about the result of all this? *That it will receive great condemnation.*

Questions for us to ponder together...

1. Why are people tempted to become self-important about matters of faith?

2. How do you think Jesus stayed humble, despite *being* God?

Chapter 68

Jesus Admires the Faith of the Poor Widow

Mark 12:41-44

41 *Jesus sat down opposite the treasury, and saw how the multitude cast money into the treasury. Many who were rich cast in much.* 42 *A poor widow came, and she cast in two small brass coins, which equal a quadrans coin.* 43 *He called his disciples to himself, and said to them, "Most certainly I tell you, this poor widow gave more than all those who are giving into the treasury,* 44 *for they all gave out of their abundance, but she, out of her poverty, gave all that she had to live on."*

Let's remember together what we read...

- Where did Jesus choose to sit down? *Across from the treasury, where people came into the Temple to give their offerings.*
- How many people did He watch while He sat there? *A great number—a "multitude."*
- How much did the wealthy people put in the box? *Much.*
- Then who came with an offering? *A poor widow.*
- How much did she put in the treasury? *Two small brass coins.*
- Who did Jesus call over to notice her gift? *His disciples.*
- According to Jesus, how much did this poor widow give? *More than anyone else who was putting money into the treasury.*
- Why does He say this? *Because the wealthy were giving out of their plenty, while she, having nothing, gave her everything.*

Questions for us to ponder together...

1. When it comes to money, what kind of reputation would you like to have with Jesus?
2. Is there something in your life that He's currently wanting you to give away?

Chapter 69

Jesus Speaks About Difficult Times to Come: Part One

Mark 13:1-10

13 *As he went out of the temple, one of his disciples said to him, "Teacher, see what kind of stones and what kind of buildings!"*

2 *Jesus said to him, "Do you see these great buildings? There will not be left here one stone on another, which will not be thrown down."*

3 *As he sat on the Mount of Olives opposite the temple, Peter, James, John, and Andrew asked him privately,* 4 *"Tell us, when will these things be? What is the sign that these things are all about to be fulfilled?"*

5 *Jesus, answering, began to tell them, "Be careful that no one leads you astray.* 6 *For many will come in my name, saying, 'I am he!' and will lead many astray.*

7 *"When you hear of wars and rumors of wars, don't be troubled. For those must happen, but the end is not yet.* 8 *For nation will rise against nation, and kingdom against kingdom. There will be earthquakes in various places. There will be famines and troubles. These things are the beginning of birth pains.* 9 *But watch yourselves, for they will deliver you up to councils. You will be beaten in synagogues. You will stand before rulers and kings for my sake, for a testimony to them.* 10 *The Good News must first be preached to all the nations."*

TO BE CONTINUED...

Let's remember together what we read...

- Where were Jesus and His friends leaving from? *From the Temple.*

- What did one of His disciples point out to Jesus? *How impressive the stones and construction of the Temple were.*

- What did Jesus say about all those important buildings? *That all of it would be torn to the ground.*

- Then where did He and His friends go? *Up on the Mount of Olives.*

- What could they see from where they were sitting? *The Temple.*

- Who then asked Him a follow-up question? *Peter, James, John, and Andrew.*

- What was their question? *When the destruction of the Temple would occur; what would be "the sign" that these things were about to happen.*

- What was Jesus' immediate warning to His friends? *"Be careful that no one leads you astray."*

- What is the false message that Jesus warns them against? *People coming in His name, claiming to be Him.*

- What did Jesus tell His friends *not* to be troubled by? *Wars and rumors of wars.*

- What are other "signs of the times" Jesus talks about? *Nations rising against each other, kingdoms fighting against each other, earthquakes, famines, and troubles.*

- What does Jesus call these outward signs? *The "beginning of the birth pains."*

- What does He tell His friends will happen to them? *They will be brought before the council (i.e. the Sanhedrin); they will be beaten; they will stand before kings and governors as witnesses.*

- Where does Jesus say the Good News must be preached? *To **all** the nations.*

Questions for us to ponder together...

1. How do you think Peter, James, John, and Andrew felt after hearing what Jesus said to them?

2. How would *you* feel if Jesus was saying these words to you today?

Chapter 70

Jesus Speaks About Difficult Times to Come: Part Two

Mark 13:11-23

11 *"When they lead you away and deliver you up, don't be anxious beforehand, or premeditate what you will say, but say whatever will be given you in that hour. For it is not you who speak, but the Holy Spirit.*

12 "Brother will deliver up brother to death, and the father his child. Children will rise up against parents, and cause them to be put to death. 13 You will be hated by all men for my name's sake, but he who endures to the end will be saved. 14 But when you see the abomination of desolation, spoken of by Daniel the prophet, standing where it ought not" (let the reader understand), "then let those who are in Judea flee to the mountains, 15 and let him who is on the housetop not go down, nor enter in, to take anything out of his house. 16 Let him who is in the field not return back to take his cloak. 17 But woe to those who are with child and to those who nurse babies in those days! 18 Pray that your flight won't be in the winter. 19 For in those days there will be oppression, such as there has not been the like from the beginning of the creation which God created until now, and never will be. 20 Unless the Lord had shortened the days, no flesh would have been saved; but for the sake of the chosen ones, whom he picked out, he shortened the days. 21 Then if anyone tells you, 'Look, here

is the Christ!' or, 'Look, there!' don't believe it. [22] For there will arise false christs and false prophets, and will show signs and wonders, that they may lead astray, if possible, even the chosen ones. [23] But you watch."

TO BE CONTINUED...

Let's remember together what we read...

- Who is Jesus talking to as He offers these words? *Peter, James, John, and Andrew.*

- Where are they sitting while they have this conversation? *On the Mount of Olives, overlooking Jerusalem and the Temple.*

- When His friends will be eventually arrested for talking about Him, how does Jesus tell them to respond? *By not being anxious or worrying about what they'll say, because the Holy Spirit will be with them and tell them what to say.*

- What are some of the sad outcomes in families that Jesus speaks about? *Brothers having brothers arrested; fathers, their children; children rising against their parents and delivering them over to death.*

- What does Jesus say to His friends about how the world will treat them? *They will be hated by all.*

- What is the phrase that is a "sign" of the end: the "abomination of _____"? *Desolation.*

- Who was the prophet who spoke of this sign? *Daniel. (Parent note: It's always helpful to make the connection that this is the Daniel of the "lion's den," etc.)*

- What are some of the terrible things Jesus talks about when He's explaining the destruction of Jerusalem? *People will be running for their lives, leaving behind everything they have; it will be terrible for women who have little children to protect; there will be much suffering and fearfulness.*

- Should the disciples be careful of "false Christs" claiming to be Jesus? *Yes, very!*

- Will these "false Christs" be somewhat convincing? *Yes, Jesus says, quite convincing.*

Questions for us to ponder together...

1. Within these frightening words, what are some promises of great comfort?

2. What do you think stood out most to Peter, James, John, and Andrew as they listened to these words?

Chapter 71

Jesus Speaks About Difficult Times to Come: Part Three

Mark 13:23b-37

23 *"Behold, I have told you all things beforehand.* 24 *But in those days, after that oppression, the sun will be darkened, the moon will not give its light,* 25 *the stars will be falling from the sky, and the powers that are in the heavens will be shaken.* 26 *Then they will see the Son of Man coming in clouds with great power and glory.* 27 *Then he will send out his angels, and will gather together his chosen ones from the four winds, from the ends of the earth to the ends of the sky.*

28 *"Now from the fig tree, learn this parable. When the branch has now become tender, and produces its leaves, you know that the summer is near;* 29 *even so you also, when you see these things coming to pass, know that it is near, at the doors.* 30 *Most certainly I say to you, this generation will not pass away until all these things happen.* 31 *Heaven and earth will pass away, but my words will not pass away.* 32 *But of that day or that hour no one knows, not even the angels in heaven, nor the Son, but only the Father.* 33 *Watch, keep alert, and pray; for you don't know when the time is.*

34 *"It is like a man, traveling to another country, having left his house, and given authority to his servants, and to each one his work, and also commanded the doorkeeper to*

keep watch. [35] *Watch therefore, for you don't know when the lord of the house is coming, whether at evening, or at midnight, or when the rooster crows, or in the morning;* [36] *lest coming suddenly he might find you sleeping.* [37] *What I tell you, I tell all: Watch."*

Let's remember together what we read...

- Who is Jesus talking to as He offers these words? *Peter, James, John, and Andrew.*

- Where are they sitting while they have this conversation? *Still on the Mount of Olives, overlooking Jerusalem and the Temple.*

- In the terrible times Jesus has been talking about, what are some of the "signs" in nature He refers to? *The sun will be darkened, the moon will stop shining, stars will fall from the sky, the universe will be shaken.*

- Then what will happen? *They will see Jesus "coming in clouds with great power and glory."*

- Then who will Jesus send out into the world? *His angels.*

- What will be the angels' job? *To gather His chosen ones from everywhere.*

- What kind of tree does Jesus then point to as a picture? *A fig tree.*

- What are the signs in a fig tree that tell you summer is near? *Its branches become tender and start producing leaves.*

- What will be the "signs" that Jesus is preparing to return? *All the wild and scary things He's been talking to His friends about.*

- What will happen before "this generation passes away"? *Those very same wild and scary things.*

- Even though heaven and earth may pass away, will Jesus' words ever pass away? *No!*

- Who is the *only One* who knows the exact hour of the end? *Only the Father—not even Jesus Himself.*

- What is the story He tells to make sure His friends keep watch? *Of a man who is traveling abroad and purposely puts his servants in charge, giving them assignments and placing a doorkeeper at the door.*

- Would those servants—would *we*, as followers of Jesus—know exactly when the master would return? *No.*

- What would be the worst way the master could find his servants? *Sleeping.*

- So what does Jesus finish by commanding? *"Watch."*

Questions for us to ponder together...

1. Do you ever stop to think that *today* could be the day when Jesus returns?

2. What is your favorite way to concentrate your heart and mind on Jesus?

Chapter 72

Jesus Is Anointed at a Dinner in Bethany

Mark 14:1-11

¹ *It was now two days before the feast of the Passover and the unleavened bread, and the chief priests and the scribes sought how they might seize him by deception, and kill him.* ² *For they said, "Not during the feast, because there might be a riot among the people."*

³ *While he was at Bethany, in the house of Simon the leper, as he sat at the table, a woman came having an alabaster jar of ointment of pure nard—very costly. She broke the jar, and poured it over his head.* ⁴ *But there were some who were indignant among themselves, saying, "Why has this ointment been wasted?* ⁵ *For this might have been sold for more than three hundred denarii,²*and given to the poor." So they grumbled against her.*

⁶ *But Jesus said, "Leave her alone. Why do you trouble her? She has done a good work for me.* ⁷ *For you always have the poor with you, and whenever you want to, you can do them good; but you will not always have me.* ⁸ *She has done what she could. She has anointed my body beforehand for the burying.* ⁹ *Most certainly I tell you, wherever this Good News may be preached throughout the whole world, that which this woman has done will also be spoken of for a memorial of her."*

---

2   300 denarii was about a year's wages for an agricultural laborer.

[10] Judas Iscariot, who was one of the twelve, went away to the chief priests, that he might deliver him to them. [11] They, when they heard it, were glad, and promised to give him money. He sought how he might conveniently deliver him.

Let's remember together what we read...

- How many days was it before the Passover week? *Two days.*

- What were the chief priests and scribes scheming about? *How to arrest Jesus and kill Him.*

- But why were they worried about doing so during the Passover? *Because the people might riot.*

- Where was Jesus at the time? *In Bethany, which is very near to Jerusalem.*

- Whose house was He in? *Simon, who formerly had had leprosy.*

- Who unexpectedly came in to the dinner? *A woman carrying a precious jar of precious oil.*

- What did she then do? *Broke the neck of the jar and poured the oil over Jesus' head.*

- Why were some of those present upset at her actions? *Because if that oil had been sold, it could've been a lot of money to give away to the poor.*

- How did Jesus respond to their grumblings? *He told them to stop it and stop troubling her—that what she'd done for Him was a good thing.*

- What did Jesus say was the difference between the poor and Himself? *That there would always be poor people for them to help—but that He Himself wouldn't be there forever.*

- What specifically did Jesus say the woman had done for Him? *Anointed His body, which was soon to be buried.*

- What did Jesus say about the remembrance of what that woman did? *That everywhere the Good News was preached, she would be remembered forever.*

- Who decided that *now* was the time to betray Jesus? *Judas Iscariot.*

- Who did he go to? *The chief priests.*

- What did they offer him for his betrayal? *Money.*

- What did Judas then start looking for? *The right time to hand Jesus over.*

Questions for us to ponder together...

1. What do you think caused that woman to do what she did?

2. What is something special and extravagant that we could do for Jesus ourselves?

Chapter 73

The Disciples Prepare the "Last Supper" for Jesus

Mark 14:12-16

12 *On the first day of unleavened bread, when they sac-rificed the Passover, his disciples asked him, "Where do you want us to go and prepare that you may eat the Passover?"*

13 *He sent two of his disciples, and said to them, "Go into the city, and there a man carrying a pitcher of water will meet you. Follow him,* 14 *and wherever he enters in, tell the master of the house, 'The Teacher says, "Where is the guest room, where I may eat the Passover with my dis-ciples?"'* 15 *He will himself show you a large upper room furnished and ready. Get ready for us there."*

16 *His disciples went out, and came into the city, and found things as he had said to them, and they prepared the Passover.*

Let's remember together what we read...

- Which day of the Passover feast was it? *The first, when they sacrificed the Passover lamb.*

- What did Jesus' friends ask Him? *Where He wanted them to go and prepare their own Passover meal.*

- How many of His disciples did Jesus send? *Two.*

- What were His instructions to these two? *Go into Jerusalem. When you see a man carrying a water pitcher, follow him. Whichever house he enters, go in and tell the owner of the house that Jesus is ready to use the room prepared for Him. The owner will then show you a large upper room all ready for the feast.*

- Did those two find things just as Jesus had described? *Yes, everything happened just as He said they would.*

A question for us to ponder together...

1. Do you remember the original Old Testament narrative of the Passover? Let's work together and re-tell ourselves what happened back then!

Chapter 74

Jesus Talks About Being Betrayed by One of His Own

Mark 14:17-21

17 When it was evening he came with the twelve. 18 As they sat and were eating, Jesus said, "Most certainly I tell you, one of you will betray me—he who eats with me."

19 They began to be sorrowful, and to ask him one by one, "Surely not I?" And another said, "Surely not I?"

20 He answered them, "It is one of the twelve, he who dips with me in the dish. 21 For the Son of Man goes, even as it is written about him, but woe to that man by whom the Son of Man is betrayed! It would be better for that man if he had not been born."

Let's remember together what we read...

- What time of day did this happen? *Evening*.

- Where did Jesus arrive with the Twelve? *To the large upper room where everything was already prepared.*

- What was the startling thing that Jesus first said over the meal? *That one of His friends was going to betray Him.*

- How did this make the disciples feel? *"Sorrowful" and sad.*

- What was the question more than one of them asked? *"Surely not I?"*

- Who did Jesus say it would be? *One of the twelve, who even shared the very dishes on that table.*

- What were the strong words Jesus said about His betrayer? *"Woe" to that person—in other words, almost like a curse—for it would be better if that man had never been born.*

Questions for us to ponder together...

1. What does it tell you about Jesus that *He knew* what was coming for Him?

2. Why do you think Judas Iscariot chose to betray Jesus?

Chapter 75

Jesus Changes the Meaning of the Passover Forever

Mark 14:22-26

²² *As they were eating, Jesus took bread, and when he had blessed, he broke it, and gave to them, and said, "Take, eat. This is my body."*

²³ *He took the cup, and when he had given thanks, he gave to them. They all drank of it.* ²⁴ *He said to them, "This is my blood of the new covenant, which is poured out for many.* ²⁵ *Most certainly I tell you, I will no more drink of the fruit of the vine, until that day when I drink it anew in God's Kingdom."* ²⁶ *When they had sung a hymn, they went out to the Mount of Olives.*

Let's remember together what we read...

- Where does the opening of this scene take place? *In the large upper room where Jesus shared the Passover meal with His friends.*

- What did Jesus hold up for His friends to look at? *The bread from the Passover table.*

- What did He do with the bread? *Blessed it, broke it, and gave it to His friends.*

- What did Jesus say about the bread? *That they should eat it—for this was His body.*

- What did Jesus take up next? *The cup holding the Passover wine.*

- What did he do with the cup? *Held it up, gave thanks for it, and handed it to His friends to drink.*

- What did Jesus say about the cup and the wine? *That this was His "blood of the new covenant, which is poured out for many."*

- What did Jesus say about His own drinking of wine? *That the next time He'd take a sip, He'd be drinking it in the Kingdom of God.*

- What did they do after the bread and the wine? *Sang a hymn of praise.*

- Then where did they go? *Out to the Mount of Olives.*

Questions for us to ponder together...

1. Why did Jesus change the meaning of the Passover feast on the night before the Cross?

2. What words that Jesus said especially stand out for you?

Chapter 76

Jesus Tells a Prideful Peter What Is to Come

Mark 14:27-31

27 *Jesus said to them, "All of you will be made to stumble because of me tonight, for it is written, 'I will strike the shepherd, and the sheep will be scattered.'* 28 *However, after I am raised up, I will go before you into Galilee."*

29 *But Peter said to him, "Although all will be offended, yet I will not."*

30 *Jesus said to him, "Most certainly I tell you, that you today, even this night, before the rooster crows twice, you will deny me three times."*

31 *But he spoke all the more, "If I must die with you, I will not deny you." They all said the same thing.*

Let's remember together what we read...

- Where were Jesus and His friends on their way to? *The Mount of Olives, having left from the upper room where they'd shared the Passover meal.*

- What does Jesus tell His friends will happen to them all tonight? *They will "stumble" because of their connection with Him.*

- What animal does the prophecy He quotes compare them to? *Sheep.*

- After His resurrection, where does Jesus say He'll meet with His friends? *Back in Galilee.*

- Who then speaks up? *Peter.*

- What does Peter say to Jesus? *In essence, "Even if everyone leaves You behind, I never will!"*

- What does Jesus tell Peter that, in fact, is going to happen? *That on that night, before the rooster crows twice, he will deny knowing Jesus three times.*

- Did Peter believe Jesus? *No! He even claimed he'd be willing to die with Jesus.*

- Did the other disciples say the same thing? *Yes.*

Questions for us to ponder together...

1. Why do you think that Peter was so sure he'd stand by Jesus?

2. How do you think Jesus felt about Peter, even though He knew about his denial-to-come?

Chapter 77

Jesus Prays Sorrowful Prayers in the Garden of Gethsemane

Mark 14:32-36

³² *They came to a place which was named Gethsemane. He said to his disciples, "Sit here, while I pray."* ³³ *He took with him Peter, James, and John, and began to be greatly troubled and distressed.* ³⁴ *He said to them, "My soul is exceedingly sorrowful, even to death. Stay here, and watch."*

³⁵ *He went forward a little, and fell on the ground, and prayed that, if it were possible, the hour might pass away from him.* ³⁶ *He said, "Abba, Father, all things are possible to you. Please remove this cup from me. However, not what I desire, but what you desire."*

Let's remember together what we read...

- Where did Jesus and His disciples arrive to? *A garden called Gethsemane on the Mount of Olives.*

- What did Jesus say to nine of His friends? *"Sit here, while I pray."*

- Which three did Jesus invite to come pray with Him? *Peter, James, and John.*

- How was Jesus feeling in this moment? *Greatly troubled and distressed.*

- What did He say to Peter, James and John? *That His soul was filled with sorrow—almost like death. And He asked that they would stay with Him and keep watch.*

- Then what did Jesus do? *He went off a little ways and fell on the ground in prayer.*

- What did Jesus pray? *That if possible He might not have to go through with the Cross.*

- What did Jesus call God? *"Abba Father." (Parent note: This would be like His praying, "Daddy! Oh, Daddy!")*

- What was the word-picture He gave for the sufferings to come? *A "cup."*

- What did Jesus say about His desires vs. God's desires? *That God's should always come before His own.*

Questions for us to ponder together...

1. How does it make you feel to see Jesus so scared, so troubled, so in need of His friends' support?

2. How does it make you feel to know that He's doing this *for you?*

Chapter 78

Jesus Prays More Sorrowful Prayers in the Garden of Gethsemane

Mark 14:37-42

³⁷ *He came and found [Peter, James and John] sleeping, and said to Peter, "Simon, are you sleeping? Couldn't you watch one hour?* ³⁸ *Watch and pray, that you may not enter into temptation. The spirit indeed is willing, but the flesh is weak."*

³⁹ *Again he went away, and prayed, saying the same words.* ⁴⁰ *Again he returned, and found them sleeping, for their eyes were very heavy, and they didn't know what to answer him.* ⁴¹ *He came the third time, and said to them, "Sleep on now, and take your rest. It is enough. The hour has come. Behold, the Son of Man is betrayed into the hands of sinners.* ⁴² *Arise! Let's get going. Behold: he who betrays me is at hand."*

Let's remember together what we read...

- Where were Jesus and His friends during this encounter? *In the garden of Gethsemane, on the Mount of Olives.*

- Who did Jesus find sleeping, even after He'd asked them to keep watch with Him? *Peter, James, and John.*

- What does Jesus say to Peter? *"Are you sleeping? Couldn't you keep watch for even an hour? Now watch and pray, so that you don't fall to temptation."*

- What does Jesus say to Peter about the "spirit" and "the flesh"? *That the spirit is willing, but the flesh is weak.*

- Then what did Jesus do? *Went away again and prayed the same words about His fear of the Cross.*

- Returning again to His friends, what did Jesus find? *That they'd fallen asleep again!*

- After praying again and returning again, what does Jesus say to His friends? *That the "hour has come"— that He is about to be betrayed.*

- Who does Jesus point out is almost there? *The one who is betraying Him, i.e. Judas Iscariot.*

Questions for us to ponder together...

1. What does Jesus mean when He says that our "spirit is willing, but the flesh is weak"?

2. As Jesus moved toward His arrest, how do you think His face and eyes looked?

Chapter 79

Jesus Is Arrested—and Deserted

Mark 14:43-52

43 *Immediately, while he was still speaking, Judas, one of the twelve, came—and with him a multitude with swords and clubs, from the chief priests, the scribes, and the elders.* 44 *Now he who betrayed him had given them a sign, saying, "Whomever I will kiss, that is he. Seize him, and lead him away safely."* 45 *When he had come, immediately he came to him, and said, "Rabbi! Rabbi!" and kissed him.* 46 *They laid their hands on him, and seized him.* 47 *But a certain one of those who stood by drew his sword, and struck the servant of the high priest, and cut off his ear.*

48 *Jesus answered them, "Have you come out, as against a robber, with swords and clubs to seize me?* 49 *I was daily with you in the temple teaching, and you didn't arrest me. But this is so that the Scriptures might be fulfilled."*

50 *They all left him, and fled.* 51 *A certain young man followed him, having a linen cloth thrown around himself over his naked body. The young men grabbed him,* 52 *but he left the linen cloth, and fled from them naked.*

Let's remember together what we read...

- Where did this whole scene take place? *The garden of Gethsemane, on the Mount of Olives.*

- Who led the people coming to arrest Jesus? *Judas Iscariot.*

- What was Judas' sign for the soldiers about who to arrest? *He would give Jesus a kiss on the cheek.*

- What did Judas call Jesus as he came forward to give Him that kiss? *"Rabbi!"*

- What did one of Jesus' disciples do in order to try and save Him? *Drew his sword and slashed off the ear of one of the soldiers. (Parent note: We know, from John's Gospel, that this was Peter.)*

- What did Jesus tell the soldiers that they were treating Him like? *A robber.*

- Where does Jesus remind them that they might've arrest Him anytime they wanted to? *When He was teaching every day in the Temple—in front of all the people of Jerusalem.*

- What did Jesus say that this arrest was the fulfillment of? *The Scriptures about His life and death.*

- Who ran away at this point? *All of Jesus' friends.*

- What (somewhat funny!) thing happened to the "young man"? *The soldiers grabbed him, getting ahold of his tunic. When it came off in their hands, he ran off naked into the night. (Parent note: There are biblical commentators who raise the suggestion that this may, in fact, have been John Mark, the author of the Gospel of Mark, himself. Hence his addition of this strange detail.)*

Questions for us to ponder together...

1. How do you imagine Jesus' countenance—the way He carried Himself—in this moment of His arrest?

2. How does it make you feel to know that He's doing this *for you?*

Chapter 80

Jesus' Trial Before the Religious Leaders

Mark 14:53-59

⁵³ *They led Jesus away to the high priest. All the chief priests, the elders, and the scribes came together with him.*

⁵⁴ *Peter had followed him from a distance, until he came into the court of the high priest. He was sitting with the officers, and warming himself in the light of the fire.* ⁵⁵ *Now the chief priests and the whole council sought witnesses against Jesus to put him to death, and found none.* ⁵⁶ *For many gave false testimony against him, and their testimony didn't agree with each other.* ⁵⁷ *Some stood up, and gave false testimony against him, saying,* ⁵⁸ *"We heard him say, 'I will destroy this temple that is made with hands, and in three days I will build another made without hands.'"* ⁵⁹ *Even so, their testimony didn't agree.*

Let's remember together what we read...

- Where did the officers of the religious leaders take Jesus? *To the high priest.*

- Who else was there waiting for Him? *All the chief priests, the elders of the people, and the scribes.*

- Who was following behind but keeping his distance? *Peter.*

- Where did Peter come to? *All the way into the courtyard of the high priest.*

- Where did Peter take a seat? *Next to a fire there in the open air.*

- What were the religious leaders trying to do as they confronted Jesus? *Find witnesses who had testimony by which to condemn Jesus.*

- Did anyone give evidence against Jesus—whether false or true? *Yes, "many." But their testimonies didn't line up with each other.*

- What was one of the testimonies we're told of? *That Jesus had said He would destroy the Temple and that, in three days, it would be rebuilt.*

- Did even this testimony agree with others? *No.*

Questions for us to ponder together...

1. Why do you think Peter came all the way to the courtyard of the high priest's palace?

2. When Jesus *did* talk about "three days" needed to rebuild the Temple, what was He *actually* talking about? (See John 2:19-22.)

Chapter 81

The Religious Leaders Condemn Jesus

Mark 14:60-65

⁶⁰ *The high priest stood up in the middle, and asked Jesus, "Have you no answer? What is it which these testify against you?"* ⁶¹ *But he stayed quiet, and answered nothing. Again the high priest asked him, "Are you the Christ, the Son of the Blessed?"*

⁶² *Jesus said, "I am. You will see the Son of Man sitting at the right hand of Power, and coming with the clouds of the sky."*

⁶³ *The high priest tore his clothes, and said, "What further need have we of witnesses?* ⁶⁴ *You have heard the blasphemy! What do you think?" They all condemned him to be worthy of death.* ⁶⁵ *Some began to spit on him, and to cover his face, and to beat him with fists, and to tell him, "Prophesy!" The officers struck him with the palms of their hands.*

Let's remember together what we read...

- Who stood up and directly confronted Jesus? *The high priest.*
- What question did he first ask Jesus? *"Have you no answer?"—meaning, "Why aren't You trying to defend Yourself?"*
- Did Jesus respond? *No, He stayed quiet.*
- Then, what did the high priest ask Jesus? *"Are you the Christ, the Son of the Blessed?"*
- What did Jesus say in response? *"I am. You will see the Son of Man sitting at the right hand of Power, and coming with the clouds of the sky." (Parent note: Jesus' first words of response are the powerful words "I AM"—which is one of the names of God from the Old Testament—see John 8:58.)*
- What did this cause the high priest to do to his priestly robes? *He tore them in anger.*
- What did the high priest then say to the Council? *"What further need have we of witnesses? You have heard the blasphemy! What do you think?"*
- What did the whole Council think? *They condemned Jesus to deserve death.*
- Then what did they do to Him? *They spat on Jesus, beat Him, slapped Him, and mocked Him.*

Questions for us to ponder together...

1. When you remember that Jesus is God-in-the-flesh, what sticks out most to you in this moment?
2. How does it make you feel to know that He's doing this *for you?*

Chapter 82

Peter Denies Jesus Three Times

Mark 14:66-72

[66] *As Peter was in the courtyard below, one of the maids of the high priest came,* [67] *and seeing Peter warming himself, she looked at him, and said, "You were also with the Nazarene, Jesus!"*

[68] *But he denied it, saying, "I neither know, nor understand what you are saying." He went out on the porch, and the rooster crowed.*

[69] *The maid saw him, and began again to tell those who stood by, "This is one of them."* [70] *But he again denied it. After a little while again those who stood by said to Peter, "You truly are one of them, for you are a Galilean, and your speech shows it."* [71] *But he began to curse, and to swear, "I don't know this man of whom you speak!"* [72] *The rooster crowed the second time. Peter remembered the word, how that Jesus said to him, "Before the rooster crows twice, you will deny me three times." When he thought about that, he wept.*

Let's remember together what we read...

- Where was Peter when all of this occurred? *In the courtyard of the high priest's palace, sitting by the fire.*

- Who first accused him of knowing Jesus? *One of the maids of the high priest.*

- What did she say about Peter? *"You were also with the Nazarene, Jesus!"*

- What did Peter say in response? *In essence, "I have no idea what you're talking about!"*

- Where did Peter then go? *Away from the others, onto the "porch" on the side of the courtyard.*

- What sound was then heard? *A rooster crowing for the first time.*

- What did the high priest's maid say about Peter, pointing him out to the others? *"This is one of them,"* meaning one of the disciples of Jesus.*

- What did Peter do? *He denied knowing Jesus a second time.*

- After a little while, what did someone else say to Peter? *That Peter was a disciple of Jesus; that clearly he was from Galilee; that his accent proved where he was from.*

- What were the first words out of Peter's mouth this time? *Curses and swearing.*

- What did he then say about Jesus? *"I don't know this man of whom you speak!"*

- What sound was then heard a second time? *The rooster's crowing.*

- What did this sound remind Peter of? *Of Jesus telling him that before the rooster crowed twice tonight he would have denied Him three times.*

- Remembering this, what did Peter do? *He wept.*

Questions for us to ponder together...

1. What do you think caused Peter to deny knowing Jesus three times on that night?

2. What do we learn about our ability to follow Jesus *in our own strength* as we watch Peter go through this night?

Chapter 83

Jesus Is Brought Before the Roman Governor

Mark 15:1-5

¹ *Immediately in the morning the chief priests, with the elders and scribes, and the whole council, held a consultation, bound Jesus, carried him away, and delivered him up to Pilate.* ² *Pilate asked him, "Are you the King of the Jews?"*

He answered, "So you say."

³ *The chief priests accused him of many things.* ⁴ *Pilate again asked him, "Have you no answer? See how many things they testify against you!"*

⁵ *But Jesus made no further answer, so that Pilate marveled.*

Let's remember together what we read...

- When did these events occur? *First thing early in the morning, on the Friday of that Passover week.*

- Who held an early morning conference? *The chief priests, the elders, the scribes, and the whole council. (Parent note: This gathering was called the Sanhedrin.)*

- What did they do with Jesus? *They bound His hands, took Him away, and brought Him before Pontius Pilate, the Roman governor.*

- What was Pilate's first question to Jesus? *"Are you the King of the Jews?"*

- How did Jesus respond? *"So you say."*

- What were the chief priests saying to Pilate? *All kinds of accusations against Jesus.*

- Hearing all this, what did Pilate ask Jesus? *"Have you no answer? See how many things they testify against you!"*

- How did Jesus respond? *He said nothing.*

- How did Pilate react? *He was amazed.*

Questions for us to ponder together...

1. Why do you think Jesus remained silent through so much of His trial?

2. From where do you think Jesus was drawing His courage during these experiences?

Chapter 84

Jesus, Pilate, and the Crowds

Mark 15:6-14

⁶ *Now at the feast [Pilate] used to release to them one prisoner, whom they asked of him.* ⁷ *There was one called Barabbas, bound with his fellow insurgents, men who in the insurrection had committed murder.* ⁸ *The multitude, crying aloud, began to ask him to do as he always did for them.* ⁹ *Pilate answered them, saying, "Do you want me to release to you the King of the Jews?"* ¹⁰ *For he perceived that for envy the chief priests had delivered him up.* ¹¹ *But the chief priests stirred up the multitude, that he should release Barabbas to them instead.* ¹² *Pilate again asked them, "What then should I do to him whom you call the King of the Jews?"*

¹³ *They cried out again, "Crucify him!"*

¹⁴ *Pilate said to them, "Why, what evil has he done?"*

But they cried out exceedingly, "Crucify him!"

Let's remember together what we read...

- What was the name of the feast week during which all of this happened? *Passover.*
- What was the Roman tradition that the governor usually did that week? *Released one prisoner, whichever the people of Jerusalem requested.*
- What was the name of the criminal who was in prison at that time? *Barabbas.*
- What had Barabbas done? *He had taken part in an effort to overthrow the government and had committed murder.*
- Who did Pilate want to release to the people? *Jesus.*
- What did Pilate sense was the cause of the chief priest's hatred of Jesus? *That they were jealous of Him and of His following.*
- What did the chief priests stir up the crowd to do? *To ask for the release of Barabbas instead of Jesus.*
- When Pilate asked the crowds what he should do with Jesus, what did they shout? *"Crucify him!" meaning, hang Him on a cross.*
- Shocked, what did Pilate ask the crowds? *"Why? What evil has He done?"*
- But what did the people keep shouting at him? *"Crucify him!"*

Questions for us to ponder together...

1. If Jesus ever met Barabbas, how do you think He would've treated him?

2. How do you imagine the look on Jesus' face as He hears those words: "Crucify Him"?

Chapter 85

Jesus Is Flogged, Mocked, and Abused

Mark 15:15-20

[15] *Pilate, wishing to please the multitude, released Barabbas to them, and handed over Jesus, when he had flogged him, to be crucified.* [16] *The soldiers led him away within the court, which is the Praetorium; and they called together the whole cohort.* [17] *They clothed him with purple, and weaving a crown of thorns, they put it on him.* [18] *They began to salute him, "Hail, King of the Jews!"* [19] *They struck his head with a reed, and spat on him, and bowing their knees, did homage to him.* [20] *When they had mocked him, they took the purple off him, and put his own garments on him.*

Let's remember together what we read...

- Where is all of this occurring? *At the palace and grounds of the Roman governor, Pontius Pilate.*

- Why did Pilate decide to release Barabbas, the murderer? *In order to please the crowds.*

- What was then done to Jesus? *He was "flogged." (Parent note: A flogging was a specialized Roman torture in which a person was stripped nearly naked, their hands tied to a post, and then they were beaten with a "cat of nine tails"—a handle with nine leather straps interwoven with bits of glass, metal, and bone. Each lashing would rip skin off the person's back. Jesus received thirty-nine of these lashes.)*

- Where did the soldiers then take Jesus? *To an inner courtyard called the "Praetorium."*

- How did they mock Jesus? *They put a purple robe around Him (purple was the color used to express royalty) and made a crown of long thorns and pressed it down on His head.*

- What did the soldiers say to Jesus? *"Hail, King of the Jews!"*

- What did they then do to Jesus? *Struck His head with a stick, spat on Him, and mockingly bowed down to Him.*

Questions for us to ponder together...

1. How do you think Jesus was able to make it through this kind of torture?

2. How does it make you feel to know that He's doing this *for you?*

Chapter 86

Jesus Goes to the Cross

Mark 15:20b-28

20 They led him out to crucify him. 21 They compelled one passing by, coming from the country, Simon of Cyrene, the father of Alexander and Rufus, to go with them, that he might bear his cross. 22 They brought him to the place called Golgotha, which is, being interpreted, "The place of a skull." 23 They offered him wine mixed with myrrh to drink, but he didn't take it.

24 Crucifying him, they parted his garments among them, casting lots on them, what each should take. 25 It was the third hour,[1] and they crucified him. 26 The superscription of his accusation was written over him, "THE KING OF THE JEWS." 27 With him they crucified two robbers; one on his right hand, and one on his left. 28 The Scripture was fulfilled, which says, "He was counted with transgressors."

1. 9:00 am

Let's remember together what we read...

- Who led Jesus up to the hill where He would be crucified? *The same Roman soldiers who'd just been beating Him and mocking Him.*

- What was the name of the man the soldiers forced to carry Jesus' cross? *Simon, from Cyrene.*

- What does Mark tell us this man's sons were named? *Alexander and Rufus. (Parent note: Biblical scholars believe that these two sons became prominent members of the first-century church, so it was a nice point of reference for readers to hear that their father had been the one who helped Jesus.)*

- What was the name of the hill where Jesus died? *Golgotha.*

- What does that name mean? *The place of the skull.*

- Did Jesus take the wine He was offered that had myrrh in it? *No. (Parent note: The myrrh was mixed into the wine to deaden the crucified person's sense and physical feeling. But Jesus purposed to experience everything of the Cross on our behalf.)*

- What did the Roman soldiers do with Jesus' clothes? *Cast lots for them so that they could each get a full piece or two.*

- What did the sign above Jesus' head read? *"The King of the Jews."*

- How many others were crucified at the same time as Jesus? *Two robbers.*

Questions for us to ponder together...

1. If you were Simon of Cyrene, forced to help Jesus with His cross, what do you think you'd have felt having that experience?

2. Why do you think Mark makes the point of telling us about the other two men who were being crucified?

Chapter 87

The Crowds Mock the Crucified Jesus

Mark 15:29-32

29 *Those who passed by blasphemed him, wagging their heads, and saying, "Ha! You who destroy the temple, and build it in three days,* 30 *save yourself, and come down from the cross!"*

31 *Likewise, also the chief priests mocking among themselves with the scribes said, "He saved others. He can't save himself.* 32 *Let the Christ, the King of Israel, now come down from the cross, that we may see and believe him." Those who were crucified with him also insulted him.*

Let's remember together what we read...

- Who were the first group of people who mocked Jesus on the Cross? *Just random people who happened to be walking by.*

- What was the mocking thing they shouted at Him? *"You said You could destroy the Temple and rebuild it in three days—well, now, save Yourself; come down from there!"*

- Who else was there mocking Jesus? *The chief priests and scribes.*

- What was it they said about Jesus? *"He saved others. He can't save himself. Let the Christ, the King of Israel, now come down from the cross, that we may see and believe him."*

- Who else was mocking Jesus? *The two robbers on either side of Him. (Parent note: In Luke's Gospel, one of the robbers has a beautiful change of heart and becomes the first person in history to believe in the work of the Cross. It would be well worth your family's time to look at that narrative too!)*

Questions for us to ponder together...

1. How do you think Jesus felt while He was dying for the broken people of this world and broken people were shouting out their mockeries of Him?

2. Why did Jesus *not* come down from the Cross; what kept Him there?

Chapter 88

Jesus Dies on the Cross

Mark 15:33-39

33 *When the sixth hour had come, there was darkness over the whole land until the ninth hour.*[3] 34 *At the ninth hour Jesus cried with a loud voice, saying, "Eloi, Eloi, lama sabachthani?" which is, being interpreted, "My God, my God, why have you forsaken me?"*

35 *Some of those who stood by, when they heard it, said, "Behold, he is calling Elijah."*

36 *One ran, and filling a sponge full of vinegar, put it on a reed, and gave it to him to drink, saying, "Let him be. Let's see whether Elijah comes to take him down."*

37 *Jesus cried out with a loud voice, and gave up the spirit.* 38 *The veil of the temple was torn in two from the top to the bottom.* 39 *When the centurion, who stood by opposite him, saw that he cried out like this and breathed his last, he said, "Truly this man was the Son of God!"*

---

3   Noon and 3:00 pm, respectively

Let's remember together what we read...

- How long after Jesus was crucified did the darkness come? *Three hours.*

- How long did the darkness last? *Three hours.*

- What did Jesus shout out at the six-hour point? *"My God, my God, why have you forsaken me?"*

- What did the people who heard this think He was talking about? *They thought He was calling for the help of the prophet Elijah.*

- What did someone offer Jesus at this point? *A sponge dipped in vinegar and held up to His lips.*

- What did Jesus do next? *Cried out with a loud voice.*

- How does Mark describe the moment of Jesus' death? *That He gave up His spirit.*

- What happened in the Temple at that moment? *The forty-foot-tall curtain between the Holy Place and the Most Holy Place suddenly ripped from top to bottom.*

- What did one of the Romans soldiers, a centurion, say when He saw Jesus' death? *"Truly this man was the Son of God!"*

Questions for us to ponder together...

1. Why did Jesus die on the Cross?

2. How does it make you feel to know that He did this *for you?*

Chapter 89

Those Who Saw Jesus Die—and Joseph, Who Asked for His Body

Mark 15:40-47

40 *There were also women watching [Jesus' death] from afar, among whom were both Mary Magdalene, and Mary the mother of James the less and of Joses, and Salome;* 41 *who, when he was in Galilee, followed him and served him; and many other women who came up with him to Jerusalem.*

42 *When evening had now come, because it was the Preparation Day, that is, the day before the Sabbath,* 43 *Joseph of Arimathaea, a prominent council member who also himself was looking for God's Kingdom, came. He boldly went in to Pilate, and asked for Jesus' body.* 44 *Pilate marveled if he were already dead; and summoning the centurion, he asked him whether he had been dead long.* 45 *When he found out from the centurion, he granted the body to Joseph.* 46 *He bought a linen cloth, and taking him down, wound him in the linen cloth, and laid him in a tomb which had been cut out of a rock. He rolled a stone against the door of the tomb.* 47 *Mary Magdalene and Mary, the mother of Joses, saw where he was laid.*

Let's remember together what we read...

- Who was standing nearby and saw Jesus' death? *Some of the women who had followed Him.*

- What were some of their names? *Mary Magdalene, Mary the mother of "James the less" and Joses, and Salome.*

- What are we told about the way these women had followed Jesus? *They "served him."*

- That evening, who went to visit Pontius Pilate? *Joseph, from Arimathea.*

- What are we told about Joseph? *That He was a "prominent" member of the Council, and that he himself had been looking for the Kingdom of God.*

- What did he ask of Pilate? *That the soldiers would let him have Jesus' body.*

- Why did Pilate "marvel"? *Because Jesus had died sooner than he'd expected.*

- Who did Pilate consult with? *One of the centurions who'd been there—perhaps the very one who'd said Jesus was the "Son of God."*

- What did Joseph do to prepare Jesus' body? *Brought a linen cloth, took Jesus' body down from the cross, and wound Him all around with the cloth.*

- Where did Joseph place Jesus' body? *In a tomb "which had been cut out of a rock."*

- What did he put over the opening? *A great stone.*

- Who watched to see where Jesus was laid? *Mary Magdalene and the other Mary.*

Questions for us to ponder together...

1. What do you think drew people to Jesus so much during His lifetime?

2. What draws *you* to Jesus so much in *your* lifetime?

Chapter 90

The Women Who Went to the Tomb and Found It Empty!

Mark 16:1-8

[1] *When the Sabbath was past, Mary Magdalene, and Mary the mother of James, and Salome, bought spices, that they might come and anoint him.* [2] *Very early on the first day of the week, they came to the tomb when the sun had risen.* [3] *They were saying among themselves, "Who will roll away the stone from the door of the tomb for us?"* [4] *for it was very big. Looking up, they saw that the stone was rolled back.*

[5] *Entering into the tomb, they saw a young man sitting on the right side, dressed in a white robe, and they were amazed.* [6] *He said to them, "Don't be amazed. You seek Jesus, the Nazarene, who has been crucified. He has risen. He is not here. Behold, the place where they laid him!* [7] *But go, tell his disciples and Peter, 'He goes before you into Galilee. There you will see him, as he said to you.'"*

[8] *They went out, and fled from the tomb, for trembling and astonishment had come on them. They said nothing to anyone; for they were afraid.*

Let's remember together what we read...

- What day had just concluded when the friends of Jesus went to the tomb? *The Sabbath—the next day, the Saturday, after He'd died.*

- Why did these two Marys come to the tomb? *They brought special spices with which they wanted to anoint Jesus' body.*

- What time of day on that Sunday did they come? *"Very early" when "the sun had risen."*

- What was the question they were asking themselves as they approached? *"Who will roll away the stone for us?"*

- What did they then see? *That the stone was already rolled back!*

- Where did they then go? *Inside the tomb.*

- And what did they see inside? *A young man dressed in a white robe.*

- How did the women feel? *Amazed—and probably quite frightened!*

- What did the angel say to the women? *That they needn't be amazed; that Jesus had risen: "He is not here."*

- What did the angel then tell the women to do? *To see for themselves the place where Jesus' body had been. Then to go and tell His disciples that they would see Him in Galilee.*

- What did the Marys then do? *The left the tomb as if running away.*

- How were they feeling? *Astonished, trembling, afraid, and excited.*

- At that time, who did they tell of their conversation with the angel? *No one, because they were afraid.*

Questions for us to ponder together...

1. Do you believe that Jesus is really, truly, actually alive *today?*

2. If we really, truly, actually believe that fact, how should we live?

Chapter 91

Almost No One Can Believe in the Resurrection!

Mark 16:9-13

9 Now when he had risen early on the first day of the week, he appeared first to Mary Magdalene, from whom he had cast out seven demons. 10 She went and told those who had been with him, as they mourned and wept. 11 When they heard that he was alive, and had been seen by her, they disbelieved. 12 After these things he was revealed in another form to two of them, as they walked, on their way into the country. 13 They went away and told it to the rest. They didn't believe them, either.

Let's remember together what we read...

- What day of the week did Jesus rise from the dead? *The "first day of the week," i.e. Sunday.*

- Who did He reveal Himself to, first? *Mary Magdalene.*

- What are we told about Mary Magdalene's first inter-action with Jesus? *That He had cast seven demons out of her.*

- Who did she go and tell about seeing Jesus alive? *The other disciples and followers, who were mourning and weeping.*

- Did they believe her? *No. They "disbelieved."*

- Who did Jesus show Himself to next? *To two of His followers who were walking in the country. (Parent note: This is a wonderful narrative—the "Road to Emmaus"— found only in Luke's Gospel.)*

- What did those two do? *Came back to Jerusalem to tell all the others.*

- Did the others believe them? *No.*

Questions for us to ponder together...

1. Why did the disciples so strongly doubt the testimony of their friends?

2. What emotions do you think the friends of Jesus were feeling all throughout that Sunday?

Chapter 92

The Risen Jesus Appears to His Friends

Mark 16:14-18

14 Afterward he was revealed to the eleven themselves as they sat at the table, and he rebuked them for their unbelief and hardness of heart, because they didn't believe those who had seen him after he had risen. 15 He said to them, "Go into all the world, and preach the Good News to the whole creation. 16 He who believes and is baptized will be saved; but he who disbelieves will be condemned. 17 These signs will accompany those who believe: in my name they will cast out demons; they will speak with new languages; 18 they will take up serpents; and if they drink any deadly thing, it will in no way hurt them; they will lay hands on the sick, and they will recover."

Let's remember together what we read...

- Who did the risen Jesus show Himself to next? *To the Eleven (i.e. the Twelve minus Judas) as they were sitting at a table—up in the upper room.*

- What did Jesus "rebuke" His friends for? *For not believing in His resurrection and for their "hardness of heart"—that they'd refused to believe the testimony of those who'd already seen Him.*

- What is His next command to His friends? *"Go into all the world, and preach the Good News."*

- What does He say about those who believe and are baptized in His name? *That they are "saved."*

- What are some of the "signs" He says will accompany their preaching? *They will cast out demons; speak in new languages; pick up snakes, unharmed; if they drink anything deadly, it won't harm them; and they will lay their hands on the sick, and those sick ones will recover.*

Questions for us to ponder together...

1. What does it mean to you to believe in Jesus and follow Him?

2. What are ways *you* can "Go into all the world, and preach the Good News"?

Chapter 93

The Risen Jesus Ascends and Hands His Kingdom to His Friends

Mark 16:19,20

[19] *So then the Lord, after he had spoken to them, was received up into heaven, and sat down at the right hand of God.* [20] *They went out, and preached everywhere, the Lord working with them, and confirming the word by the signs that followed. Amen.*

Let's remember together what we read...

- Forty days after the Resurrection, what happened to Jesus? *He was lifted back up to Heaven; He "ascended."*

- Arriving back unto Heaven, where did He take a seat? *At the right hand of the Father.*

- What did Jesus' disciples do? *Went out from Jerusalem and preached everywhere.*

- Did their preaching go well? *Yes! The Lord Jesus was working with them (and through them!) and He confirmed their preaching with amazing signs and miracles.*

Questions for us to ponder together...

1. What does it mean to you that Jesus is alive—and still seated upon the Throne of Heaven—right now, today?

2. What sorts of miracles would you like to see happen during your lifetime?

About Eugene Luning

Eugene Luning directs The Union, a ministry within the New Horizons Foundation, which exists for teaching, retreats, podcasting and spiritual counseling in Colorado and around the country. Additionally, he is the cofounder of a real estate technology company, Panoramiq Markets Inc. Eugene and his wife Jenny are the parents of three children, Hadley, Tripp and Hoyt. They live in Colorado Springs, Colorado, where they also lead a weekly fellowship, The Anchor.

From
Bill Johnson & Eugene Luning

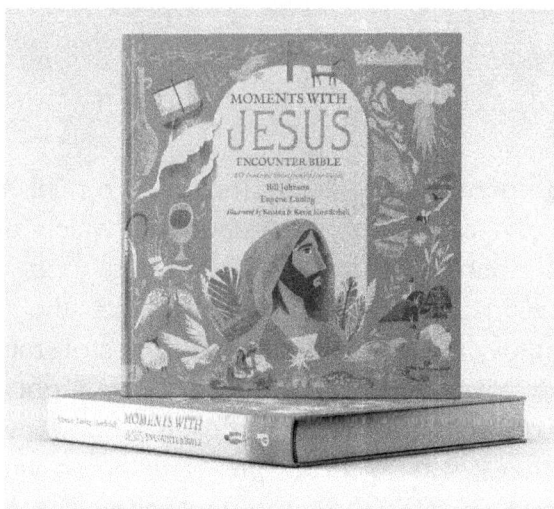

Let Jesus capture your child's imagination!

If you are looking for a resource to help introduce your child to Jesus, look no further. The *Moments with Jesus Encounter Bible* was designed to help kids encounter Him for themselves!

What makes the *Moments with Jesus Encounter Bible* different from other children's Bibles?

While other children's Bibles contain informative stories from the Old and New Testaments, the *Moments with Jesus Encounter Bible* puts kids in the middle of the action of twenty essential stories from the four Gospels. Through dynamic, first-hand storytelling, kids come face to face with the Living Word Himself, getting a clear picture of who Jesus is, what He is like, and His love for them *personally*.

The Moments with Jesus Encounter Bible combines masterful storytelling with captivating artwork to create an imaginative, biblical encounter like no other. Presented in a simple, beautiful format, the *Moments with Jesus Encounter Bible* will help you shepherd your kids into a thriving, dynamic relationship with Jesus.

What are you waiting for? Start your adventure today!

Purchase your copy wherever books are sold